Lawyer health and wellbeing: How the legal profession is tackling stress and [illegible] resiliency

EDITED BY ALEX DAVIES

Commissioning editor
Alex Davies

Published by ARK Group:

UK, Europe and Asia office
5th Floor
10 Whitechapel High Street
London, E1 8QS
United Kingdom
Tel: +44(0) 207 566 5792
publishing@ark-group.com

North America office
4408 N. Rockwood Drive, Suite 150
Peoria IL 61614
United States
Tel: +1 (309) 495 2853
publishingna@ark-group.com

www.ark-group.com

Printed by Canon (UK) Ltd, Cockshot Hill, Reigate, RH2 8BF, United Kingdom

ISBN: 978-1-78358-390-4

A catalogue record for this book is available from the British Library

ARK Group is a division of Wilmington plc. The company is registered in England & Wales with company number 2931372 GB. Registered office: 5th Floor, 10 Whitechapel High Street, London E1 8QS.

VAT Number: GB 899 3725 51.

Contents

Executive summary

Recent years have witnessed growing concern internationally in wellbeing and mental health across the legal community, a shift reflected in a host of initiatives, networks, reports and research studies. Changes to working patterns, generational shifts, and an increased interest in overall wellbeing have contributed to a growing movement towards better working practices – across all industries but particularly in high pressure professions such as law. In his introduction to this book, Richard Martin of byrne·dean and formerly a partner in Jones Day and Speechly Bircham, describes his own experience of mental illness and recovery, reminding us of the vital role that lawyers have to play in our increasingly complex world. He highlights some of the particularities of lawyers and legal practice that might give rise to mental health problems, and why this is important. The introduction provides insight into what organizations should be doing to enhance and maintain the mental health of their people and an overview of the topics covered in the chapters that follow.

The genesis of the lawyer wellbeing movement in the United States has spread to the UK, EU, Canada and Australia. In chapter one, Bree Buchanan, ABA Commission on Lawyers Assistance Programs, covers the 2016 research regarding lawyer and law student impairment that served as the catalyst for creating the National Task Force on Lawyer Wellbeing. From this coalition of national organizations came the 2017 Report, which in turn launched a wide variety of national and state policy and practice innovations. Bree summarizes a snapshot of those developments.

Chapter two focuses on the importance of emotions in the legal workplace. Emma Jones, senior lecturer at the University of Sheffield Law School, explains how being able to identify, understand, regulate and use emotions within legal work can assist lawyers in developing psychologically healthier and more sustainable ways of working. Examples of this include the role of emotions in assisting interactions with colleagues, enhancing client care skills and assisting individuals in identifying the affective cues that provide important messages about their own (and others) wellbeing. The chapter emphasises the need for lawyers to become reflective practitioners in order to develop key emotional competencies and concludes by discussing models of reflection that can be used to provide accessible and effective ways to embed emotional reflexivity within the working practices of legal professionals.

In chapter three, Kate Dodd, diversity and inclusion consultant at Pinsent Masons LLP, explains the Mindful Business Charter – a collaboration (initially) between leading banks and law firms committed to driving change in how these two typically high-stress industries work. Kate explains why the Charter is needed, how its founders came together as a group of lawyers and clients to put it together, how it is being implemented at Pinsent Masons LLP and how they are spreading the word across the industry.

The impact of workplace mental health in the law is not new; we are just talking about it more now. Chapter four, by Elizabeth Rimmer, discusses the origins of LawCare, a UK-based charity that provides information and support to the legal community. The world of work is changing with the rise of AI and machine learning. The human skills of the lawyer – trust, empathy, and judgment – will be more valued in the future legal workplace, so it's imperative that young lawyers are prepared for this. Recruitment and retention is already a challenge in the law and succession plans need to take into account different expectations of future generations. LawCare's role is to provide support, information and resources around this culture change, challenging stigma, encouraging people to speak up, and identifying the practical steps that individuals and workplaces can take now. Mental health is of massive importance to a successful organization, creating workplaces where people can thrive and do their best work.

Conversations that matter is about having conversations in the workplace when you are concerned about someone else's mental health. Although important, these conversations can be difficult and may be delayed or avoided. Chapter five, by Lubna Gem Arielle, corporate facilitator and applied theatre practitioner, explores practical steps for having conversations about mental health using a four-step-model as a framework of support. This theme continues into chapter six, in which, starting with his own story of how byrne·dean was founded, Matt Dean discusses the concept of psychological safety, and changing culture, conversation by conversation.

Chapter seven summarises and analyses the research undertaken by the Junior Lawyers Division of The Law Society of England and Wales into the negative stress and mental ill health experienced by junior lawyers in the profession. Kayleigh Leonie looks at the causes and effects of the stress that junior lawyers are experiencing and considers the positive measures that are being put in place by individuals and firms to alleviate that stress, many of which are included in the recommendations set out in The Law Society's best practice guidance for employers on supporting wellbeing in the workplace. This chapter also draws upon the insights obtained through a series of roundtables held with city law firms from 2018–2020 to explore best practice.

Chapter eight continues this focus on junior lawyers, presenting the findings of a recent study of anxiety in law funded by the mental health charity *Anxiety UK*. Richard Collier, professor at the university of Newcastle, connects these discussions to growing concerns about law students in legal education and training, the nature of the transition into legal careers, and considers whether, with regard to addressing the issue, wellbeing might usefully be characterized as a "wicked problem" in the legal profession.

Supervising without stress explores the relationship of complex parts in which supervisors and those they supervise experience. At its core is having to treat each other with care and to work on the relationship itself. Get it right and you build loyalty, trust and teamwork. Get it wrong and you destroy trust and can end up trying to second guess those involved with destructive and self-destructive consequences. Using the analogy of your first love, chapter nine by Paul Bennett at Bennett Briegal LLP explores how supervisors can become more effective, those supervised can help their supervisors, and in a lighthearted way, how to address supervision in law firms. The underlining message is there are two parties in the relationship; and both need to work at it as a mutual blame game helps no one.

Lawyers are treated far more harshly when misconduct occurs than doctors, nurses and other professionals such as accountants. In chapter ten the judicial approach that the Solicitors Disciplinary Tribunal and the Courts take to mental health is explored within the legal profession. Since 2018 the position has hardened as the High Court has restricted the discretion shown by the Tribunal, which has found itself increasingly fettered in a series of controversial cases. Paul Bennett, who has acted for solicitors facing serious mental health issues linked to misconduct, including controversial cases, explores the key lessons and poses a question for regulators: Have we got the health/misconduct balance wrong? A mix of case law and lessons to be learnt is explored in the context of lawyer health and wellbeing.

James Pereira QC, a barrister at FTB Chambers, is fairly rare in the sense that he is both a successful practising lawyer and also a professional coach for individuals and organizations. James got into coaching as a result of his own personal journey, which was aimed at trying to figure out how to be a high performing lawyer and also maintain wellbeing. What he found was that focusing on wellbeing actually improved his professional ability, as well as his wellbeing. Part personal story, part practical advice based on actual experience, in this chapter James gives practical insights into lawyer wellbeing, and explains how wellbeing interventions that support personal mastery can be used to upskill lawyers to perform better in mainstream legal practice.

Our final chapter deals with brass tacks. Renee Branson, founder of RB Consulting, asks why it is that, despite a greatly increased awareness of the scale of the mental health problem within the legal profession, it still persists. There must be, she argues, a continued appeal to the moral and ethical case for improving the wellbeing of lawyers and other professionals who are negatively impacted by an often-punishing career. It truly is the right thing to do. But, she also acknowledges, that altruistic appeal must be coupled with a solid business case and vetted leadership that provides justification for long-term financial and structural investments in wellbeing.

About the authors

Lubna Gem Arielle is a corporate facilitator/applied theatre practitioner who designs and delivers leadership training for law firms including mental health and workplace wellbeing. Her focus on mental health awareness and advocacy emerged from her lived experience of clinical depression and anxiety. In response to a need to foster supportive environments, Lubna developed a conversational model (NILE) to elicit open and effective workplace communication about mental health. She is the creative director of Bridging the Blue, a Virtual Reality work made in collaboration with computer scientists at Trinity College, Dublin, exploring the potential of VR to facilitate empathic and non-judgmental listening. Lubna has an interdisciplinary background which includes 12 years as a solicitor (CMS, FieldFisher, PwC and head of legal at London, arts centre, Rich Mix) as a legal educator making CPD programs, as a writer/presenter for Legal Network Television (a subsidiary of the University of Law) in parallel with lecturing on MA programmes in arts management at Birkbeck, University of London and Sotheby's Institute of Art. Towards the end of her traditional legal career, Lubna studied fine art at Central Saint Martins, which evolved into performance and then applied theatre practice. All of these converged into her work as a corporate facilitator/applied theatre practitioner. She is a qualified executive coach with a focus on positive psychology and wellbeing and is a mental health first aider and trained in SafeTalk.

Paul Bennett, partner at Bennett Briegal LLP, is a specialist in both professional practice and employment law work. Paul is a nationally recognized expert who can help if the situation is challenging or potentially career-defining. Paul works across England and Wales, with London and Manchester dominating as the locations of key regulators. Paul has acted in a series of high profile cases involving professionals, especially lawyers and doctors, in which mental health has been a factor. An experienced advocate with a track record of winning complex cases, he has also written three books for lawyers on compliance and regulation.

Renee Branson is the founder and principal at RB Consulting. Combining 20 years in education, counseling, and non-profit leadership, her passion and purpose is helping individuals, teams, and organizations cultivate resilience. After years of working with survivors of trauma she now teaches others the skills of resilience for workplace wellbeing.

As a certified resilience coach (CReC), she provides clients with immediately usable tools to increase resilience, wellbeing, and optimism in the workplace. She works with lawyers, educators, business professionals, non-profit leaders, and others to help them understand and incorporate resilience in their own professional lives and in the teams they lead.

Renee is a member of the American Bar Association's Attorney Wellbeing Committee. Renee speaks to international audiences on resilience and wellbeing, including as a guest lecturer at the UCLA School of Law. She holds an MA in counseling psychology from the University of Colorado and a BS from The Ohio State University.

Bree Buchanan is founding co-chair of the National Task Force on Lawyer Wellbeing and is a co-author of its groundbreaking 2017 report, *The Path to Well-Being: Practical Recommendations for Positive Change.* Bree is chair of the ABA Commission on Lawyers Assistance Programs which works to ensure assistance is readily available for those in the legal community experiencing issues related to substance use or mental health issues. As director of the Texas Lawyers Assistance Program from 2013 until retirement in 2018, she regularly worked with individual lawyers experiencing these issues, and with legal employers who were seeking resources and support for their staff. Her tenure with that program followed a two-decade legal career that included positions as a litigator, lobbyist and law professor. She is now senior advisor with Krill Strategies LLC, providing consultation on issues related to lawyer wellbeing and impairment for major legal employers. Bree is a frequent speaker for international and national law-related organizations, as well as global law firms on strategies for lawyer wellbeing and impairment. In 2018, she was awarded the "Excellence in Legal Community Leadership Award" by Hazelden Betty Ford Foundation. She has shared her own story of recovery as a featured guest on podcasts in the United States and Canada, and her writing has appeared in *Law Practice Today, Judicature* and *Family Lawyer Magazine.* In 2018, she graduated from the Seminary of the Southwest with a Masters in Spiritual Formation, where she honed a deep interest in the intrinsic link between meaningful work and personal wellbeing, as well as in assisting individuals with vocational discernment. Bree tends to her own wellbeing by engaging in a regular meditation practice, cycling, rowing, and being willing to ask for help when she needs it.

Richard Collier FAcSS FRSA is a professor of law at Newcastle University, UK. He has published widely in the area of law and gender and has recently been the recipient of a Leverhulme Trust Fellowship in connection with the project *Wellbeing, Law and Society: Politics, Policy and Practice*. He is presently writing a book on wellbeing in the legal community for Cambridge University Press and has just conducted research funded by *Anxiety UK* (2018) into experiences of anxiety amongst junior lawyers. His previous work has addressed family law, fatherhood, criminology, the legal profession and legal education and research and books include: *Men, Law and Gender* (2010), *Fragmenting Fatherhood: A Socio-Legal Study* (with Sally Sheldon, 2008), *Masculinities, Crime and Criminology* (1998), *Masculinity, Law and the Family* (1995) and *Fathers' Rights Activism and Law Reform* (ed. 2007). Richard is an editorial board member of *Social and Legal Studies: An International Journal*. He is presently researching masculinities in the world's legal professions and undertaking a project on men and gender equality in universities.

Matt Dean's central purpose is to help people understand the impact they have on others. His first book, *The Soft Stuff: reclaiming kindness for the world of work* was published in 2019. He's worked with employment problems since 1989, initially as a lawyer in City law firms.

In 2003 he left Simmons & Simmons, where he had created a team that talked to people in client organizations about the risks they were running and the impact they were having on others. With Victoria Byrne he created byrne.dean, a consultancy dedicated to creating kinder, fairer, more productive workplaces. Matt's best known for his inspiring facilitation; he's done his 10,000 hours. He challenges people to recognize their power, focus on their impact and change their bit of the workplace. He's worked in 28 countries and is equally at ease with the most senior leaders or large, all staff groups. Inclusion and diversity has been a big part of his work since 2004. Two head and neck cancers in 2009 and 2016 shaped his life and inform his work.

Kate Dodd is a diversity and inclusion consultant for Pinsent Masons LLP. She advises the firm, and its clients, on a full range of wellbeing, culture and inclusion topics. Kate's passion is for creating great workplaces that allow talent to thrive. She has a flair for culture change and helping leaders to learn how to start conversations around complex workplace issues. Kate has been instrumental in founding and developing the Mindful Business Charter, which is a cross-industry cultural change enabler focused upon increasing wellbeing. The MBC has now been adopted by more than 40 international organizations, creating happier, more mindful workplaces. Kate is passionate about supporting businesses to attract and retain the best talent, and to cultivate the skills needed to serve their clients and communities. Known for managing complex issues with sensitivity and discretion, Kate is described as "very knowledgeable with a great understanding of clients' businesses".

Kate is an employment lawyer by background. An experienced advocate, she has represented her clients in Employment Tribunals across England, Scotland, and Wales across a full range of sensitive discrimination and equality issues.

Dr Emma Jones is currently a senior lecturer at the University of Sheffield Law School, developing modules on digital lawyering and lawtech. Prior to that she was a senior lecturer and teaching director at the Open University Law School. She is also a senior fellow of the Higher Education Authority and an associate academic fellow of the Honourable Society of the Inner Temple. Emma's research focuses on the role of emotions and wellbeing in legal education and the legal profession. She is academic lead on the Fit for Law project, working with the charity LawCare, to provide free online resources for legal professionals promoting emotionally and psychologically healthier ways of working. Prior to moving into academia, Emma was a solicitor in private practice, specialising in construction law.

Kayleigh Leonie is a solicitor specialising in employment law and a trustee of LawCare, a registered charity that supports good mental health and wellbeing throughout the legal community. Kayleigh has undertaken research, written articles, and published best practice guidance for employers on supporting the wellbeing of their employees on behalf of the Law Society of England and Wales. Kayleigh holds regular roundtables for employers to share best practice on supporting wellbeing in the workplace.

Richard Martin is a director of leading workplace consultancy byrne·dean. Richard spent the first 20 years of his career as an employment lawyer in London, serving as a partner at Gouldens and then Jones Day (following the merger of those firms) before moving to Speechly Bircham where he ran the large employment team and sat on the firm's management committee. In 2011 he suffered a serious mental breakdown, spent time in hospital and two years recovering. He is now a leading activist in the field of mental health. His day-to-day work involves working with organizations around the world to raise awareness of mental health and illness, enabling people to be more aware of their own wellbeing, creating supportive cultures in which wellbeing can be discussed, and ensuring that those in difficulty are supported. He co-chairs the Lord Mayor of London's This is Me campaign, which uses storytelling to reduce the stigma around mental health and illness, and he leads the Mindful Business Charter, an initiative to remove the unnecessary stress in our workplaces. Richard is a mental health first aid instructor and coach. In 2018 he published his memoir of mental illness and recovery, *This too will pass – Anxiety in a professional world.*

James Pereira QC is a practising barrister and coach. He was called to the Bar in 1996 and took silk in 2014, and is a tenant at Francis Taylor Building, Inner Temple, London. He is the co-author of several leading textbooks in his field of practice, and listed as a leading QC in both the Legal 500 and Chambers and Partners Directory of the UK Bar. As a coach, he works with individuals, teams and organizations. He is an NLP Master practitioner, a trained organizations and relationships systems coach, systemic constellations coach, and a member of the International Coaching Federation. He co-writes a regular column in *The Lawyer*, "Loving Legal Life", and is a regular public speaker in the field of leadership, wellbeing and performance in the legal profession. He is a co-founder of The Libra Partnership (www.thelibrapartnership.com) and Gather Coaching (www.gathercoaching.com)..

Elizabeth Rimmer started her working life as a solicitor specializing in clinical negligence. She has been managing and developing charities in the mental health sector for over 15 years, and joined LawCare as chief executive in 2015.

Introduction

By Richard Martin, director, byrne·dean

The last few years have seen an explosion of interest in mental health generally, but specifically in the legal profession. My own involvement in the subject began abruptly in May 2011. At that point I was 40 years old, a father of three young children, a partner in a London law firm, running a large employment law team, and sitting on the firm's management committee. It seemed like I was your archetypal success story.

I went away for a week with my family. On the way back from the holiday, driving around the Boulevard Périphérique south of Paris, I experienced what I now know was a panic attack and never went back to my law firm. I descended rapidly into an increasingly anxious and depressed shadow of my former self until I was admitted to psychiatric hospital for a month, followed by the best part of another two years getting back to a state of mind that allowed me to contemplate slowly, and oh so carefully, re-engaging with the world of work.

To me, and most of the people around me at the time, it seemed to happen almost overnight. Of course, it wasn't really like that. It was simply that I did not have the self-awareness or understanding to notice what was happening to me. Like far too many people before and after me, I ignored the few symptoms I was dimly aware of, and carried blindly on, assuming that, somehow, this would all sort itself out in the end if I could just get through the next day, the next week, the next year. That blindness was only heading in one direction, particularly if I carried on behaving as I was. I was fortunate that my legal career afforded me access to some fantastic support to pick up the pieces.

It is this experience, its impact upon my family and me, and what I have learned about myself and mental health as a result, that informs my passion for the subject and is why I am so honored to be asked to introduce this vital and timely book.

This is a book about lawyers. Some of what it says is unique to lawyers. Just as, however, not all lawyers or law firms are the same and we should be careful not to over-generalize, it also true that many of the issues that lawyers face apply equally to other professions – it is not just lawyers and those that work and live with them that would benefit from reading this book with an open and enquiring mind.

Lawyers often get a bad press. How many jokes are told about lawyers? How many stereotypes are cast? Sadly, in my experience, too many of these jokes and stereotypes are put about by lawyers themselves. One of the things that frustrates me about lawyers is that they do not think they matter, they do not think they are important, they do not think they are worth looking after, or that if they are, they should come at the end of a very long list of other priorities. And when they reach that point in their to-do list, they lack the self-awareness, energy, and time to do anything about it.

On the one hand, particularly when focusing on an individual lawyer, this can seem like naïve self-sacrifice, something to be pitied perhaps – these lawyers are, after all, just trying to do their best. When viewed at a macro level, however, when there seems to be an awareness across an entire profession that things are fundamentally flawed, but where the profession appears to profess an inability or unwillingness to do anything about it, it can begin to seem negligent.

Lawyers matter. And when I say lawyers, I do not mean the law as a concept or a profession, or even law firms or in-house teams. I mean individual lawyers.

It is lawyers that uphold and enforce the rule of law and hold government to account. Lawyers are the people who help protect the environment, society, and each of us from powerful businesses and individuals. It is lawyers that help to enable commerce, whether on a global level, negotiating vast mergers and acquisitions, or navigating the complexities of the financial markets, or when I want to sell my house. Lawyers help us when we have to deal with the practicalities of the death of a family member, or the trauma of family breakdown. Lawyers are the people who deal with (often harrowing) criminal cases, whether prosecuting or defending those accused. It is lawyers that help us when we are injured in accidents or abused in our workplaces. The law, and the rule of law, is fundamental to so many aspects of our lives and it is lawyers who help us navigate that, often at the most difficult and challenging times of our lives.

Beyond the narrow confines of their legal work, lawyers will often be looked to for leadership and guidance on broader ethical and moral issues – both in-house lawyers and those in private practice will often find themselves acting as a moral compass for the organizations they advise.

At the same time, lawyers are people. They are mothers and fathers, sons and daughters, sisters and brothers. They have friends and colleagues, bosses, and people reporting to them. They matter to all these people too and they in their turn have emotions and needs.

The first thing too many lawyers need is the self-respect and courage to say that they and their wellbeing matter. And now more than ever we need, as a profession, to be taking our mental health and wellbeing seriously. There is a mental health crisis across society. The last few years have highlighted that the legal profession is no exception to that. In our first chapter, Bree Buchanan discusses the research done by the ABA in the US. The worrying picture that emerges there is mirrored in the Law Society of England and Wales Junior Lawyers Division's (JLD) research referenced in chapters seven and eight by Kayleigh Leonie and Richard Collier. That this is not a new phenomenon is clear from the decades of work done by LawCare in the UK, to which its CEO, Elizabeth Rimmer, refers in chapter four.

It is clear that lawyers are experiencing mental health problems at an alarming rate, far above the already worrying levels across society as a whole. This demands attention and action on a human, moral level. Lives are being destroyed, those of the lawyers that suffer and also, too often, those of their loved ones. At the extreme is suicide, very often the result of someone getting to such a point of mental anguish and/or despair that they do not feel able, or willing, to carry on living. Mental illness does not have to reach that point, however, for its impact to be profound.

This crisis also demands attention and action because of the demands of legal practice itself. The provision of legal advice is often (although admittedly not always) complex and challenging. The issues at stake and the arguments involved may make it so, as does the context for the clients involved, and often the clients themselves. We turn to lawyers when issues really matter to us, often at a deeply emotional level, and we ask those lawyers to help us navigate those fraught and choppy waters with clarity and the highest degrees of cognitive functioning, level headedness, and ethics.

And at the same time as a lawyer is dealing with our issue, s/he is also dealing with many other, no doubt equally demanding, issues and clients, juggling priorities, moving seamlessly during the day from dealing with one matter to another. And when your matter is closed and you have moved on from the urgency and intensity of whatever your lawyer was helping you navigate, hopefully to a calmer place, s/he has moved on to the next issue, the next client, the next crisis.

Lawyers generally work under a degree of pressure and many will need a certain level of pressure to operate at their best. We will all have our Goldilocks zone, where the pressure is enough but not too much, neither too hot nor too cold, but it may not take much to drift beyond that to a point where things are getting too much, when we begin to feel stressed. Lawyers can also experience stress when there isn't enough pressure, when there isn't enough work to do and they start worrying about what that means for them, their career and whatever else. Tim Cantopher in his landmark book *Depressive Illness – the curse of the strong* describes stress or anxiety-induced depression as one of the most common causes of depression for professionals generally – when persistent stress eventually causes even the strongest of minds to crack.

Stress is a problem because when the pressure gets to that point our flight/fight response can be so triggered that vital oxygen- and energy-rich blood is diverted away from our brains to the muscles in our arms and legs, enabling us to run away or fight more effectively. That is a helpful mechanism when the anxiety is being triggered by a physical predator. It is less helpful when the very thing that is causing us anxiety – the legal work we have to get done for example – requires our brains to be operating at their best.

If lawyers are stressed and anxious, they will find it more difficult to do the thinking their work requires, which is likely to impact the quality and/or effectiveness of their work. Equally, some of the common symptoms around depression, a very common mental illness, include indecision, inability to focus, memory problems, confusion and loss of judgement – none of which are going to help with the provision of complex legal advice.

So we need lawyers, but critically we need lawyers who are mentally healthy. Understanding mental health, knowing what good mental health is, being sufficiently emotionally literate to recognize a deterioration in our mental health, and having the language and culture to be able to talk about it, are critical for lawyers to be able to take better care of themselves and those around them. In chapter two, Emma Jones looks at the importance of emotional literacy in the context of the provision of legal services and also how this emotional literacy must be applied to lawyers themselves. In chapter five, Lubna Gem Arielle looks at how we can have better conversations around mental health.

One of the more effective ways of creating conversation around any sensitive issue, and of breaking down stigma, is through the power of storytelling. I am privileged to co-chair the steering committee for the Lord Mayor of London's This is Me campaign, which harnesses that power to break down the stigma around mental illness. Ordinary people telling their stories, through film or written word, create the space for conversation. They engage people on a human, emotional level, they give permission for people to talk and they help others realize that what they are experiencing is not unique, that they are not alone, that it is OK. Many businesses, including many law firms, have seen huge changes in the culture around mental health through this simple, and age old, art.

When I published my memoir of my experience of mental illness and recovery, *This Too Will Pass – Anxiety in a professional world*, I was asked, pre-publication, how I felt about my experience becoming so public. My reply was that I felt naked. The wise person who asked me that question said she understood that feeling but perhaps I could think of it that, by writing my book, I was giving other people clothes.

Raising awareness of the issue and having conversations is important but we can go much further – after all, much of what lawyers do is concerned with the assessment, management, and apportionment of risk. What is it about lawyers and the law that is causing these alarming rates of mental illness? I have alluded already to the high pressured environment in which many lawyers operate. Lawyers, like other professionals, are trained to put the interests of others before their own and they are often consumed by perfectionism and the fear of making a mistake.

In the training we do at byrne·dean we will often look at the unconscious thinking patterns that can lie at the heart of common mental disorders – catastrophizing, black and white thinking, personalization and more. When we look at what things cause us angst, and why, we will often find a number of these unhelpful and limiting beliefs at play. While many people experience these thinking patterns to some extent, for many lawyers they are their daily bread and butter. And we know that the human brain likes habits – the more we do something, or the more we think in a particular way, the more likely it is we will do that same thing, think that same way, again. If these negative thinking patterns are part of being a lawyer, unless we are careful and unless we have sufficient self-awareness, the more we do law the more we are at risk of thinking in these ways in all aspects of our lives, greatly increasing our chances of developing mental health problems. It is, after all, the way we think about something, rather than the thing itself, that causes us to feel anxiety or stress, even if that thinking is unconscious.

The JLD research to which I have referred shows that over the few years of that study the situation has been getting worse. I am sure that some of that will be down to greater awareness within society generally, as well as a greater willingness to talk about it – those are welcome trends of course. My belief is that other factors are also at play. When I look back to the start of my legal career, which was not that long ago, I did not have a computer on my desk. I am not sure we had what we would now call a computer in the office at all. Communications came to me in the post, once, or sometimes twice, a day. We did have faxes but they were cumbersome and labor intensive (you had to have fax operators) and so tended to be used only for really urgent letters. I had a telephone (which of course required me to be at my desk to use), but only my secretary had the number for it. I had an office, with a door I could close. These all contributed to a working environment that was more controlled, more predictable and in which I had the autonomy to create the space and time to think – to do the clever stuff that lawyers need to do. And when I left the office at the end of the day, whenever that was, I left. I might take something home with me to read or mark-up but I was not still connected, on call.

That way of working would seem alien to the lawyers now entering the profession, with communication dominated by 24/7 email which they can, and often are expected to (whether by themselves or others), access 24/7. Clients and colleagues have their direct lines and mobile phone numbers. Clients communicate by text and WhatsApp messages, colleagues through chat tools, as well as email. If an email does not get responded to immediately then it is followed by a phone call or a text. How conducive is that environment to the cognitive reflection required of a lawyer? The job of lawyering has not changed that much (and nor has the design of the brains that do it), but the environment in which it is done has changed completely.

I like metaphors. I recently visited someone who kept a horse in a paddock out the back of their house. Having admired the horse, my attention turned to the high quality timber fencing that divided the paddock up into lots of smaller spaces. Why have you gone to such great expense, I asked, to divide the paddock up in this way? Apparently, if you put a horse in a field of lush long green grass, it may carry on eating that grass until it makes itself ill, often through laminitis. So we create smaller spaces to protect them. That made me think about lawyers – if you put an average lawyer in a field of lush long green work, s/he will often carry on working until s/he makes her or himself ill. We used to have lots of fences in place to protect lawyers – the office, 9 to 5 and other such restrictions. The last few decades, through the ubiquity of IT, have resulted in all those fences being taken down.

I am no Luddite. IT brings amazing benefits but, like all things, it has a flip side when not used carefully. No one ever stopped to ask whether it would be a good thing for lawyers to be on call 24/7, answering emails when they are disturbed in the night, interrupting their family time to speak to clients and more, but that is where too many of the profession have drifted. It feels like perhaps we need to give people back the autonomy and courage to re-erect some fences, to re-establish some boundaries.

There is much that can be done about the culture of law firms themselves. In chapter six, my colleague and the co-founder of byrne·dean, Matt Dean, discusses the idea of psychological safety and how we can create workplace cultures that provide this. If we accept that the business of doing law creates its own inherent risks, then surely we should be making the environment in which we practice as safe as possible – health and safety is not just about physical issues. That will also, of course, enable lawyers to be as effective in their thinking as possible. Healthy lawyers work more effectively.

And for as long as I have been a lawyer there has been a constant refrain around the end of the billable hour, although its demise still seems some way off. It has always seemed to me to be a fairly blunt, inaccurate, and counter-intuitive way to assess the value of a lawyer's contribution. At the same time, the ever increasing targets set for chargeable (and non-chargeable) hours require individual lawyers to be accounting for their every working minute, which must place considerable stress on them – certainly, time recording is often cited as a cause of workplace stress by lawyers. And those five or six minute units all feed into an accounting machine that values the firm's success solely in terms of its profits per equity partner, without reference to the real purpose of the underlying work. Reconnecting lawyers with their purpose and measuring success in those terms would, I am sure, make for better wellbeing.

I have mentioned the research that shows the scale of the crisis affecting the profession as a whole. One of the things law firms and legal teams could do better is measure what is happening across their organizations. Engagement surveys, pulse surveys, absence records, insurance claims, use of employee helplines and many more sources could be used to measure levels of mental health and wellbeing, or problems around mental illness, allowing targeted action to be taken to address issues that arise, as well as measuring the impact of interventions taken to improve things.

It is worth mentioning some other areas of internal activity that many law firms are looking at. One of the consequences of the lack of awareness and the stigma around mental illness is the fear of any issue being medicalized. Creating a network of colleagues across an organization who are clearly signposted as ambassadors, champions or mental health first aiders – people like us that we can go and talk to without having to take the step of approaching a professional, or even human resources or our boss – can make it far easier for someone to access help and support at an early stage.

At the same time, many organizations provide in-house counselling or psychological support – having access to that support within my building, without having to externalize something, call an insurer or phone my doctor, seems to make it more likely that we will access effective help at an early stage – and all the evidence suggests that the earlier issues are addressed, the less likely they are to develop into a serious problem and the more quickly they will be resolved.

Finally, alongside awareness raising, and training around quality conversations, there is a lot of focus on what is loosely called resilience. This is not about building superhuman lawyers, and it is not about putting the responsibility for mental health and wellbeing solely on the individual. What these programs do focus on, however, are ways in which we can all in different ways prepare ourselves as well as possible for the demands our work and lives place upon us – or, put more positively, enable us to thrive. Diet, exercise, and sleep are all relevant factors, as is emotional literacy to which I have referred, as well as understanding the way we think, to catch unhelpful thinking patterns, and adopting a more mindful way of being.

These supports are worthy and important interventions, but it is crucial that they are not perceived by the organization or the individual lawyer as making that individual solely responsible for their mental wellbeing. It does not excuse the imposition of excessive pressure and demands, nor bullying or other toxic behavior. Mental health problems must not be seen to be the result of an individual not being sufficiently resilient. As one lawyer remarked to me in a training session, "Don't talk to me about the mindfulness class being run in the boardroom at lunchtime when I haven't been home in three days and am wondering if I have time to go to the bathroom".

On that note, although it is not something covered in this book, it would be remiss not to make at least passing reference to the legal responsibilities employers in the UK have in relation to mental illness. Employers have obligations to create safe working environments and they have a duty of care in respect of their employees which may give rise to liability for mental illness, particularly if the employer is aware or should be aware of the vulnerability of an individual employee. Employers also have responsibilities under the UK's Equality Act not to discriminate against people with various protected characteristics, including disabilities. Many mental illnesses will constitute a disability for these purposes and there is also a positive duty to make reasonable adjustments to accommodate employees with a disability within the workplace. These duties require responsible people in the business to have a working knowledge of mental health and the willingness to engage in appropriate and supportive conversations about it.

Much of the valuable work being done around the mental health and wellbeing of lawyers, and more broadly, is internally focused – internal to the organization and also internal to the individual. In 2018, a number of banks and leading law firms in the UK came together to create the Mindful Business Charter. This initiative, discussed in chapter three by Kate Dodd of Pinsent Masons, one of the three original architects of the Charter, encourages discussion and collaboration between organizations. It seeks to create a framework and culture in which supplier and client can openly, and without fear, collaborate and learn from each other to remove the unnecessary sources of stress in the ways in which we work. Focused around four basic, and common sense, pillars, the Charter has ambitions to create healthier, as well as more productive, working arrangements. It is an initiative that is growing both within the UK and internationally, in the legal profession and beyond, and is something we at byrne·dean are proud to be leading.

This book therefore comes at a critical time for the legal profession – a time when the demands on the profession and the toll those demands make are greater than ever, but also a time when our awareness is finally awakening. And with that awareness is coming responsible thought and action. There is a long way to go. We are very much in a crisis still. The profession needs to look critically at itself and what it is doing to its members, and urgent action is required. It feels, however, that this may at least be beginning to happen.

Chapter 1: The lawyer wellbeing movement in the US

By Bree Buchanan, JD[1]

While attending the 2016 ABA Annual Meeting in San Francisco, leaders of three national legal organizations commandeered an empty conference room and committed to the creation of a movement that would transform the wellbeing of our profession. On that day (5 September), we agreed to focus our efforts on igniting a culture change in the legal system as to how it not only addressed behavioral health impairments (such as substance use and mental health disorders), but also how it impacted the overall wellbeing of all its members. We knew that bringing such a seismic and systemic shift would likely take a decade – or more. Our greatest fear was that no one would pay attention to our call for change. Never in our greatest imaginings could we have envisioned the speed and extent to which this movement would take hold. This chapter tells the story – the why, how, and to what end – of the National Task Force on Lawyer Wellbeing,[2] its groundbreaking report, and call to action to the legal profession.

Why create a National Task Force on Lawyer Wellbeing?

Two studies were published in 2016, each highlighting the disproportionate rates of behavioral health disorders and deep resistance to seeking help in a different group comprising the legal profession. The CoLAP and Hazelden Betty Ford Foundation study of nearly 13,000 currently-practicing lawyers (the "Lawyer Study") found that between 21 and 36 percent qualify as problem drinkers, and that approximately 28 percent, 19 percent, and 23 percent are struggling with some level of depression, anxiety, and stress, respectively.[3] Notably, this study found that younger lawyers in the first ten years of practice and those working in private firms experience the highest rates of problem drinking and depression. It also highlighted the extreme reluctance of those suffering to access any sort of assistance or treatment, primarily due to stigma, shame, and fear of being "found out". Almost immediately after publication, a flurry of articles appeared in US legal media outlets.[4]

Meanwhile in 2016, the first major study regarding the behavioral health concerns among law students was published. In 2014, over 3,300 law students from 15 law schools participated in the Survey of Law Student Wellbeing.[5] It found that 17 percent experienced some level of depression, 14 percent experienced severe anxiety, 23 percent had mild or moderate anxiety, and six percent reported serious suicidal thoughts in the past year. As to alcohol use, 43 percent reported binge drinking at least once in the prior two weeks and nearly one-quarter (22 percent) reported binge-drinking two or more times during that period. One-quarter fell into the category of being at risk for alcoholism for which further screening was recommended. Aptly named *Suffering in Silence*, the published study also highlighted the reluctance of students to seek help when experiencing these types of distress, primarily due to the stigma that surrounds these conditions and the belief that accessing resources to address a condition could negatively impact their ability to gain admission to the Bar or to find employment. For example, 42 percent of respondents believed that they needed help for mental health problems in the last year, but only half of those received counseling of any sort.

The eight people, including myself,[6] who gathered at the September 2016 ABA meeting, were motivated by these two new national studies that clearly demonstrated the unacceptably high rates of depression, anxiety and problematic drinking among US lawyers and law students, and by the long-held knowledge that too many members of the profession were functioning below their ability. As leaders of three national organizations that regularly dealt with those suffering from behavioral health impairments – the National Organization of Bar Counsel (NOBC), [7] the Association of Professional Responsibility Lawyers (APRL)[8] and the ABA Commission on Lawyers Assistance Programs (CoLAP)[9] – we realized that heightened awareness brought by the studies created a window of opportunity for action. Now, we firmly believed, was the time to create systemic changes that could address the unacceptably high rates of behavioral health conditions and lift up those in the legal profession who, though not yet experiencing impairment, were not living up to their potential.

How did the NTF start the lawyer wellbeing movement?

Immediately following the brainstorming session in San Francisco, the three founding organizations set out to build a broad-based coalition. Our goal was to create an entity that included representation from other national associations with an interest in lawyer impairment, ethics, regulation, and leadership of the profession, as well as representatives from the malpractice carriers and authors of the two catalyzing studies. Under our original name, the Wellbeing Task Force (with an irreverent wink at the resulting acronym) began developing a plan for bringing that goal to fruition. First, we determined that decisions would be made by consensus. We also affirmatively decided to forego creating a formal organizational structure, a decision that was motivated by a firm belief that too many lawyers and law students were suffering (and some even dying) such that time was of the essence. In short, members believed the profession to be at a tipping point, moving in a direction that was "incompatible with a sustainable legal profession".[10] We coalesced around this sense of urgency and were bound together by our passion to change the culture of our profession.

By November, a plan had emerged, one that called for an ambitious report that outlined the levels of distress now clearly identified by the two studies that made the case for why wellbeing and the lack thereof were existential concerns of the profession and that set forth a comprehensive definition of wellbeing for the legal community. The heart of the report would ultimately provide 44 recommendations that set out a path to both address impairments of those suffering and provide for heightened wellbeing for all members of the profession. As to the object of those recommendations, we quickly decided that our report would not be directed to the individual lawyer. We each knew – and expected all other members of the profession knew – that we needed to eat healthy foods, exercise, etc. to be our best selves. To bring about systemic change we had to direct our recommendations to those with the authority to bring about such broad-based change. This would require involvement of leaders of the profession; specifically, the leaders of stakeholder groups that governed, educated and supported lawyers, law students, and judges. These included judges, regulators, employers, law schools, bar associations, professional liability carriers, and lawyers assistance programs. Authors pointed out that the lawyers assistance programs had been – almost single-handedly – doing much of the work to both support lawyers suffering from impairments and to provide education on wellbeing strategies to the profession, and called upon other stakeholders to now share the burden. The report would also begin with a series of global recommendations that applied to all stakeholder groups, such as taking action to bring an end to the stigma associated with behavioral health conditions, taking responsibility for becoming a part of the solution, and fostering collegiality, among others.

Over the course of nine months following the initial brainstorming session in San Francisco, our passion to create a movement drove us to work long hours, with assigned tasks often shoehorned in between other work and family commitments. In fact, work session phone calls were often prefaced by comments as to the irony that working to improve the wellbeing of the profession actually required us to engage in the kind of "burning the candle at both ends" work ethic that we were trying to change. Along the way, realizing that our grassroots movement was beginning to take off, we changed our name to the more official-sounding National Task Force on Lawyer Wellbeing. In San Francisco, I had taken the role as scribe, but after the retirement of one of the two co-chairs, I stepped into that position, joining James C. Coyle of Colorado. Founding task force members recruited additional representatives from the Conference of Chief Justices, National Conference of Bar Examiners, ABA Center for Professional Responsibility and Law Practice Division, and a major national malpractice carrier.[11] An editor-in-chief, Anne Brafford, was drafted from our ranks to distill the writing of many authors and their work groups into one cohesive, concise, and compelling document.

In August 2017, the groundbreaking report, *The Path to Lawyer Wellbeing: Practical Recommendations for Positive Change* ("the Report") was published to greater success and fanfare than we could have anticipated when gathering one year before. Within days of its publication, the Conference of Chief Justices passed Resolution 6, stating their support of "the goals of reducing impairment and addictive behavior, and improving the wellbeing of lawyers, and recommends that each jurisdiction considers the recommendations of the Report of the National Task Force on Lawyer Wellbeing."[12] Almost immediately after this endorsement, the American Bar Association passed a similar Resolution at the 2017 Annual Meeting.[13] Legal media coverage was extensive and laudatory.[14] Our clarion call to the profession, it seemed, was being heard.

The Path to Lawyer Wellbeing: Practical Recommendations for Positive Change

As drafters of the Report, we knew that systemic change would occur only if we could make a powerful argument for why the stakeholders to whom it is addressed should pay heed to its recommendations. Our rationale rested on a three-fold assertion that taking on the lack of wellbeing in the profession would advance organizational effectiveness (i.e. profitability), promote ethical integrity, and – most important to us – was the humanitarian thing to do. By effectively addressing impairments, such as substance use disorders and mental health problems, and by promoting overall wellbeing, leaders of the various stakeholders in the profession could improve professionalism, protect the public, and preserve the rule of law – while also enhancing both quality of life and profitability of law practice.

The Report also set out a clear and comprehensive definition of the thematic term, wellbeing. Drawing upon the World Health Organization's definition, the term is intentionally broader than simply the absence of disease or impairment. The Report instead establishes wellbeing as "a continuous process toward thriving across all of life's dimensions: intellectual, spiritual, physical, social, emotional, and occupational".[15] The emotional dimension entails the recognition of the importance of emotions and developing flexibility in how and when emotions are expressed, as well as seeking help for mental health problems when they arise. Occupational wellbeing concerns the cultivation of personal satisfaction, growth, and enrichment in one's work, while the intellectual dimension regards continuous learning and challenging activities that promote ongoing development as essential to wellness. The spiritual dimension references the inherent human need to develop meaning and purpose in one's life. Getting regular physical activity, good nutrition, adequate sleep and rest while minimizing use of addictive substances comprises the physical dimension, while fostering a sense of connection and belonging through networks is key to the social dimension.

Our initial efforts to promote the Report and its recommendations were focused heavily on the judiciary, calling upon the chief justice of each state supreme court to convene its own task force of stakeholders. Specifically, the Report sets out a "to do" list for each chief justice in Appendix A, encouraging her or him to gather leaders of stakeholder groups, review the Report, assess which recommendations should be implemented for their state, and create an action plan to do so. My co-chair, James C. Coyle, and I were given the chance to make our case directly to the chief justices at their mid-year meeting in January 2018. Stepping on to the platform in front of an audience comprised of these esteemed jurists, I was overcome with the outright audacity we had to give them a "to do" list! It was, however, one of our most successful strategies. Numerous jurists were convinced by our arguments and, impressed with the breadth and depth of the Report, they returned to their home state to do exactly as we had asked.

The lawyer wellbeing movement is launched

State implementation of Task Force recommendations

The first states to convene a supreme court-led task force were Virginia, Massachusetts, and Vermont.[16] Other states have followed, often with a task force or committee being co-convened by the supreme court and the state's bar association. Using the Report as a springboard, at the time of this writing, well over half the states have formed working groups or task forces, revised regulations related to CLE programming and to bar admissions, commissioned studies, hosted wellbeing summits, or reallocated funds to enhance the wellbeing and support services offered to members of the profession.[17] Members of the NTF have traveled to many of these states, offering consultation and facilitation to help launch new initiatives. A primary function of the NTF today is to host regular calls for representatives of state wellbeing groups, allowing them to share strategies, challenges, and accomplishments.

An exemplary model of a state lawyer wellbeing task force can be found in the work of Virginia. Chief Justice Donald W. Lemons, an early member of the NTF, enlisted Justice William C. Mims to convene and oversee work of the 25-member Committee on Lawyer Wellbeing of the Supreme Court of Virginia. In 2018, they published their report, *A Profession at Risk*,[18] a document that has served as a guide for other states. The state's lawyers assistance program benefitted greatly from the committee's work, going from a mostly volunteer-run organization to a fully-funded and staffed program that serves the needs of lawyers, law students, and judges experiencing substance use and mental health disorders, as well as providing wellbeing support to all members of the state's profession. The Supreme Court also hired a full-time wellness coordinator to develop and promote professional health initiatives and serve as a liaison with their state's assistance program. These initiatives were funded through a $30 annual assessment for lawyers in the commonwealth. Following publication of *A Profession at Risk*, the Virginia State Bar president, Leonard C. Heath Jr., convened a special committee to identify the specific aspects of the practice of law that serve as risks to a lawyer's wellbeing. Released in 2019, *The Occupational Risks of the Practice of Law*[19] categorized the risks as physical, mental, and emotional, adaptation to 21st century practice, and those which prevent lawyers from flourishing ("self-actualization risks").

At the end of 2018, under the leadership of Chief Justice Paul Reiber, Vermont published its Action Plan[20] after a year's work by committees representing the profession's stakeholders. Over the course of 2019, Massachusetts[21], Arkansas[22], and Utah[23] published reports of their wellbeing task forces' work. Other states' task forces working towards publishing their findings and recommendations in 2020 include West Virginia, Texas, Colorado, and Hawaii.

American Bar Association and other US initiatives

For several years, Patrick Krill, lead author of the Lawyer Study discussed above and NTF member, had sought a sponsor for a wide-ranging initiative to focus major legal employers, especially global firms, on the problems identified in that study. In September 2017, immediately following the ABA's resolution in support of the Report, ABA President Hilarie Bass formed the Working Group to Advance Wellbeing in the Legal Profession.[24] The group quickly adopted Krill's project and launched the Legal Employer Pledge, a seven-point framework designed to address the profession's troubling rates of substance use and mental health disorders, as well as promote the wellbeing of all lawyers. Signatories commit to providing ongoing education regarding these disorders, "disrupting the status quo of drinking-based events," providing confidential access to resources, as well as developing policies and protocols to support assessment and treatment of behavioral health conditions.[25] Over 180 global firms, law schools, bar associations, governmental agencies, corporate general counsels and other legal employers have signed the pledge.[26]

The ABA created resources to support employers signing on to the Pledge, as well as other entities interested in joining the lawyer wellbeing movement. Under the auspices of the ABA Working Group, Anne Brafford, editor of the Report, created the Wellbeing Toolkit for Lawyers and Legal Employers.[27] This booklet provides extensive tools and practical guidance on creating a plan for either one's self or one's firm focused on wellbeing enhancement. CoLAP produced a video campaign designed to highlight personal recovery stories of lawyers, judges, and law students, serving to raise awareness about the nature of addiction and mental health distress in the profession, and challenging the biases and stigma that surround those problems. The first video, *Fear Not: Speaking Out to End* Stigma, features a diverse group of lawyers, a judge and two law students who openly talk about the challenges with behavioral health issues, including depression, anxiety, alcoholism and drug addiction, their recovery and the vital importance of asking for help.[28]

A collaborative project between the NTF and the ABA's CoLAP and Law Practice Division, the inaugural national Lawyer Wellbeing Week is being held during the first week of May 2020. The aim of this project is to raise awareness and encourage action across the profession to improve wellbeing for lawyers, law students, and judges, as well as their support teams. On each day, a different dimension of wellbeing is highlighted, with an array of activities, downloadable graphics, and videos provided to support organizations wanting to create their own event.[29]

Scholarship and research

The Report consistently underscored the importance of ongoing research and assessment of constituent groups' rates of impairment, overall wellbeing, and the efficacy of strategies and interventions undertaken toward improvement of those measures. In response, CoLAP's Law School Committee sponsored a nationwide Law School Wellness Survey in 2018 with responses from half of US law schools. The research was summarized by author and researcher, Jordana Alter Confino, in *Where Are We on the Path to Law Student Wellbeing? Report on the ABA CoLAP Law Student Assistance Committee Law School Wellness Survey.*[30] The research reveals the great strides made by many schools in areas such as orientation programming, mindfulness, and physical fitness offerings, as well as ongoing collaboration with lawyer assistance programs. Moreover, a handful of schools have emerged as trailblazers in this arena, developing innovative courses and programs designed to promote holistic wellbeing, and devising creative strategies for engaging all members of the law school community in these endeavors.

Unlike for lawyers and law students, no comprehensive research existed for the US judiciary. Consequently, the Report recommended that "CoLAP and other concerned entities conduct a broad-based survey of the judiciary to determine the state of wellbeing and the prevalence of... burnout, compassion fatigue, mental health, substance use disorders, and help-seeking behaviors".[31] In 2019, researchers conducted the Judicial Survey on Stress and Resiliency, designed to identify stressors unique to the judiciary, how those stressors affect individual judges, and strategies that judges have utilized to assist them as they pursue their work from the bench. The survey's design and resulting research paper were done by a coalition involving CoLAP, the National Judicial College, the ABA Judicial Division, and the National Center for State Court's Center for Judicial Ethics. The results, to be published in a 2020 special edition of the ABA's *The Professional Lawyer*, will assist in clarifying areas for support, education, and services, as well as implications for stress management and resiliency skills. Modelling the NTF Report, this paper also includes recommendations made to the multiple stakeholders who comprise, regulate, and support the US judicial system.

Conclusion

When the eight original members of the NTF gathered in September 2016, we recognized the opportunity presenting itself in finally having extensive research to conclusively show the disproportionate rates of behavioral health impairments in the legal profession. We knew that we had a finite window of time in which to highlight these results and to take aggressive action designed to bring systemic change to the way "business as usual" was conducted. What we did not know was the extent to which lawyers, law students, and the judiciary would awaken to and heed our clarion call for action.

To draw from the Report's closing words, "[t]o preserve the public's trust and maintain our status as a self-regulating profession, we must truly become 'our brothers' and sisters' keepers,' through a strong commitment to caring for the wellbeing of one another, as well as ourselves".[32] Across the United States, this commitment and the resulting culture change being brought by those who are joining in the lawyer wellbeing movement shows promise for a better and more sustainable future for the legal community.

References

1. Bree Buchanan, JD, MSF, is a founding co-chair of the National Task Force on Lawyer Wellbeing, an author of its Report, and a frequent speaker on wellbeing and the legal profession. She is a senior advisor with Krill Strategies, LLC. Ms Buchanan finished her three-year term as chair of the ABA Commission on Lawyers Assistance Programs in 2020.
2. See the National Task Force on Lawyer Wellbeing website at http://lawyerwellbeing.net.
3. P. R. Krill, R. Johnson, and L. Albert, "The Prevalence of Substance Use and Other Mental Health Concerns Among American Attorneys", 10, *Journal of Addiction Medicine*, 46 (2016). To access this study: https://journals.lww.com/journaladdictionmedicine/Fulltext/2016/02000/The_Prevalence_of_Substance_Use_and_Other_Mental.8.aspx
4. To see a collection of news articles and other coverage of the Lawyer Study, go to: www.americanbar.org/groups/lawyer_assistance/research/colap_hazelden_lawyer_study/
5. J. M. Organ, D. Jaffe, and K. Bender, "Suffering in Silence: The Survey of Law Student Wellbeing and the Reluctance of Law Students to Seek Help for Substance Use and Mental Health Concerns", 66, *Journal of Legal Education*, 116 (2016). To access this study: https://jle.aals.org/home/vol66/iss1/13/
6. Representing the ABA's Commission on Lawyers Assistance Programs: Terry Harrell, Linda Albert, and Bree Buchanan; for the National Organization of Bar Counsel: Paul Burgoyne, Jim Coyle, Tracy Kepler;

and for the Association of Professional Responsibility Lawyers: Barbara Rosenberg and Charles Gruber.

7. National Organization of Bar Counsel (NOBC) is a non-profit organization whose members work in the regulation of the practice of law, including lawyer and judicial discipline, legal and judicial ethics and education, promotion of professionalism, and the unauthorized practice of law. See www.nobc.org/
8. The Association of Professional Responsibility Lawyers, a non-profit organization, is comprised of lawyers, law professors, and judges holding an interest in lawyers' professional responsibility, legal ethics, legal malpractice, and the evolving law of lawyering, primarily through the application of the rules of lawyer ethics to the practice of law. See https://aprl.net/about-aprl/
9. The American Bar Association's Commission on Lawyers Assistance Programs has jurisdiction over matters relating to the advancement of wellbeing for the legal community, and the provision of professional assistance and resources to all members of the legal community struggling with depression, anxiety, stress, substance abuse or alcoholism, and other conditions that impair their professional responsibilities and interfere with their wellbeing.
See www.americanbar.org/groups/lawyer_assistance/
10. *The Report of the National Task Force on Lawyer Wellbeing, The Path to Lawyer Wellbeing: Practical Recommendations for Positive Change* 2017, introductory letter, https://lawyerwellbeing.net/the-report/
11. At the time of this writing, the following organizations have also joined: National Association of Law Student Affairs Professionals, National Client Protection Organization, and the National Council of Lawyer Disciplinary Boards. The National Association of Bar Executives and the National Council of Bar Presidents are under consideration.
12. Resolution 6 of the Conference of Chief Justices can be found at: www.americanbar.org/content/dam/aba/administrative/lawyer_assistance/ls_colap_conference_of_chief_justices_resolution_6.pdf
13. Resolution 105 of the American Bar Association can be found at: www.americanbar.org/content/dam/aba/administrative/lawyer_assistance/ls_colap_2018_hod_midyear_105.pdf
14. A partial list of news coverage, journal articles, podcasts, CLE programs, etc. can be found at: www.americanbar.org/groups/lawyer_assistance/task_force_report/. Unfortunately, during early coverage of the Report, the press routinely conflated the NTF with the American Bar Association, incorrectly assigning credit for the Report to the latter organization.
15. *The Report*, p.9.
16. Their task force reports can be found at: https://lawyerwellbeing.net/resources-2/
17. An interactive map showing state initiatives can be found at the bottom of the landing page at: https://lawyerwellbeing.net/

18. www.courts.state.va.us/programs/concluded/clw/2018_0921_final_report.pdf
19. www.vsb.org/docs/VSB_wellness_report.pdf
20. https://lawyerwellbeing.net/wp-content/uploads/2019/09/Vermont-CWBLP-State-Action-Plan-Finalwithedits132019.pdf
21. https://lawyerwellbeing.net/wp-content/uploads/2019/07/Massachusetts-SJC-Steering-Committee-Lawyer-Well-Being-Report-July-2019.pdf
22. https://lawyerwellbeing.net/wp-content/uploads/2019/10/Arkansas-Task-Force-on-Lawyer-Well-Being-Report-ADOPTED_.pdf
23. www.utahbar.org/wp-content/uploads/2019/07/Task-Force-Report-2.pdf
24. The Working Group continued as a presidential initiative of Bob Carlson, and then functions were transferred to CoLAP, where it will be an ongoing project with oversight of the Pledge Campaign.
25. A slide deck outlining the pledge can be found at: www.americanbar.org/content/dam/aba/administrative/lawyer_assistance/ls_colap_working_group_pledge_and_campaign.PDF
26. www.americanbar.org/content/dam/aba/administrative/lawyer_assistance/ls_colap_working_group_pledge_and_campaign.PDF
27. www.americanbar.org/content/dam/aba/administrative/lawyer_assistance/ls_colap_well-being_toolkit_for_lawyers_legal_employers.authcheckdam.pdf
28. www.americanbar.org/groups/lawyer_assistance/profession_wide_anti_stigma_campaign/
29. https://lawyerwellbeing.net/lawyer-well-being-week/
30. https://papers.ssrn.com/sol3/papers.cfm?abstract_id=3374976
31. *The Report*, p.32.
32. Ibid, p.47.

Chapter 2: **Emotional competence for wellbeing**

By Emma Jones, Sheffield University

Why emotional competence?

The idea that lawyers can, and should, use emotions in their work is not always an easy one to accept. Legal education and training commonly focus on the importance of neutrality, objectivity, and rationality in legal work. Emotions are commonly perceived as irrational and subjective, leading lawyers to view them as inappropriate or unnecessary in their working lives. Within legal practice, the emphasis is often on projecting a strong and emotionless professional persona. For a fledgling lawyer, it will quickly become clear that clients do show emotions, particularly in areas such as family and criminal law. However, lawyers may well pride themselves on remaining emotionless, even within highly emotive and challenging situations.

This perception of emotions, and the resulting lack of acknowledgment and use of emotions by lawyers, contradicts a large body of scientific evidence that demonstrates that emotions are an integral part of people's processes of thinking, reasoning, decision-making, and judgement. As such, they play an important and necessary role within all areas of our lives, including the legal workplace.[1] In fact, lawyers are not and should not be emotionless. Although it is appropriate to put aside your own emotions at specific times (such as when dealing with an upset client), it is not possible, or healthy, to do that in every workplace situation. It means ignoring or suppressing the valuable information, cues, and guidance that emotions can provide.

The focus of this chapter is on how being able to identify, understand, regulate, and use emotions within legal work can assist lawyers in developing psychologically healthier and more sustainable ways of working. There are various terms that describe utilizing emotions in this way, such as "emotional intelligence" or "emotional literacy", but the phrase "emotional competence" is the one used in this chapter to convey the importance of upskilling yourself in this way.[2] In relation to wellbeing, developing your emotional competence can assist you in identifying and responding to the emotional cues or "early warning signals" that help you to monitor and preserve your own emotional wellbeing. It can also assist you in understanding the actions and attitudes of colleagues and clients.

Thinking about emotions

To use emotional competence to assist with your emotional wellbeing, it can be useful to ask the following questions.

What emotions am I feeling?

This may seem obvious, but it can be difficult to interpret on occasion. What is seemingly one emotion can, in fact, be composed of a variety of different feelings and emotions. For example, when dealing with a client who is refusing to accept your advice, you may feel yourself starting to get angry. In fact, if you pause to reflect on this sense of being "angry" you might find that it is a mixture of frustration, wounded pride, and worry that your client is going to make a poor decision. Understanding these elements can help to diffuse your anger and encourage you to focus your attention on the most appropriate actions, such as ensuring your client is fully appraised of the consequences of ignoring your advice.

Sometimes, a strong emotion can also overwhelm or obscure other emotions, leading to them being ignored. For example, it is common to feel happy and elated after successfully resolving a client's claim. This can give you the boost needed to move on to the next file. However, focusing solely on this sense of happiness may obscure the other emotions involved in getting to this point. For example, you may overlook the worry and anxiety you experienced when you had to forego hobbies and leisure time to negotiate the finer details of the settlement. If these aspects are forgotten in the elation of the moment, then the important messages they are giving you will also go unheeded. Identifying these other emotions can help you to ensure that in future you set appropriate boundaries, build in time for relaxation, and practice good self-care techniques in future cases to avoid being over-stretched.

Spending some time thinking about the emotions that you have experienced during your working day will help you become better at identifying which emotions have been present and the different elements that may be involved. It will also help you to discern the differing intensities of each. One way to become more skilled at discerning different emotions is to begin to incorporate elements of contemplative practice, such as mindfulness meditation, within your day. Although these are about being "in the moment", they can also promote greater self-awareness. There are various free apps you can download to help you get started with this.[3]

Why am I feeling these emotions?

Once you have established that you are feeling a particular emotion or emotions, you need to understand why you are feeling them and what they are telling you.

Sometimes this can be as simple as an emotional cue that you are hungry, thirsty, or tired. For example, if you are feeling more worried than usual about a fairly routine matter, it is worth reflecting on your recent sleep patterns and whether tiredness is causing a more intense emotional reaction. This may seem straightforward, but it can be easy to lose sight of these basic needs. Legal work is often fast-paced and relentless, which means good nutrition and healthy sleep patterns can be difficult to maintain. Becoming more aware of these indications can help you to refocus your attention on such fundamental needs. The evidence suggests that they play a fundamental role in supporting wellbeing and shouldn't be ignored.[4]

At the other end of the scale, it may be that your emotions are, in fact, telling you something more complex or tricky to absorb. For example, if you are feeling hostile towards a judge during a trial, it could be that some of these emotions represent a form of transference, projecting unresolved feelings about parental authority onto a different figure of authority. If a client you are representing in the case is projecting their anxieties on to you and seeking reassurance, you may find you practice forms of countertransference, by "shutting down" emotionally and trying to minimize interactions. Although it is important to have healthy boundaries, failing to engage with the client's emotional responses could also lead to you being unable to recognize them as a person and acknowledge their wants and needs within the litigation process.[5]

Sometimes, obtaining a greater understanding of your emotions can be a challenging or painful process (and if this is the case you should always reach out to seek help).[6] However, by understanding your emotions you can start to unpack when, how and why they are impacting on your wellbeing.

How should I deal with these emotions?

Becoming more in tune with your emotions will help you to determine how to respond to them. For example, if you realize you always get bad tempered around 11am because you're hungry, you can take practical steps to combat that by eating a snack and not scheduling challenging meetings or interviews for that time. If you do find yourself becoming angry with a client or colleague around that part of the day, you will be able to recognize that it's likely to be a cue about hunger rather than an emotion connected to your actual work.

At other times, you may find the emotions you are experiencing are integral to your work. For example, if you make a decision in a meeting then later begin to feel a sense of unease or unhappiness, that could well be a cue to revisit the reasoning and judgements behind it, to ensure the choice made is robust and appropriate. If you feel yourself emotionally withdrawing from a needy client, that could be a cue to reflect on how this shift in approach will impact on your representation and advice going forward, and think about appropriate coping strategies to maintain healthy boundaries whilst also retaining a sense of empathy and rapport.

Developing the skills to understand how and when to regulate your emotions is important in terms of emotional wellbeing. Instead of viewing your emotions as a distraction, or being concerned that they are inappropriate or misleading, you can instead begin to see emotions as a valuable part of your working life. Using your emotions in this way means working in a psychologically healthier and more sustainable way. Trying to ignore or suppress emotions for the whole of your working life is very unlikely to work. It can be exhausting, stressful, and extremely unproductive. Recognizing the importance and value of emotions means you can use and learn from them whilst regulating them when necessary.[7]

Thinking about other people's emotions

Each client, colleague, and other individual who you interact with during the working day will also be experiencing a similar range of emotions to you. It is important to be aware of this so that you can put their behaviors and responses towards you into context.

As with your own emotions, some of these people's emotions will be incidental to their work. For example, your line manager may seem to be unhappy with your performance in a team meeting, but it could be that they have had a difficult journey into work or a row with their spouse. However, others may be integral to that individual's decision-making and professional judgement, for example, if a line manager senses a change in atmosphere in a room after a decision has been made and pauses to give time for others in the meeting to open up the discussion again if they wish to do so.

In the case of colleagues, you may well be able to spot emotional cues when their wellbeing is deteriorating or at risk. For example, if a usually calm and cheerful colleague is unusually snappy or dismissive, this can be a sign that something is wrong. If they begin speaking unusually quickly and seem agitated over small issues, this could also indicate high stress levels. If an efficient colleague begins to miss deadlines or avoid discussing particular issues, this can once again signal that they are in need of additional help and support. To be able to spot that such reactions and responses are out-of-the-ordinary, it is important to be aware more generally of the emotional temperature of your workplace and the usual ways in which your colleagues display and deal with emotions. This once again requires you to be able to identify and understand emotions (this time in other people).

It is also important to consider how your own emotional reactions and responses may impact on others' emotional states. For example, if you are a lawyer in a challenging legal workplace with difficult deadlines and pressure to achieve billing targets it can be easy to forget small social niceties such as saying please or thank you. Research has highlighted that a lack of civility can be an issue for lawyers.[8] Being in an environment where people are disrespectful, or even downright rude, can be damaging to people's long-term emotional wellbeing. Maintaining an awareness of the impact of seemingly small behaviors such as this can be a simple but effective way to contribute to a more positive working environment.

Using emotions in managing others

For lawyers with management responsibilities, it is particularly important to be aware of the emotional states of the colleagues who you manage. This may seem like an additional burden, but in fact it will enable you to respond proactively to situations where someone's wellbeing is affected. In the long-term this is more effective and efficient than having to deal with the consequences retroactively, at a point where that person's professional performance and personal life are likely to have been significantly impacted.

As a manager, you are also in a position where you can model appropriate behaviors to others around you. Some lawyers have been trailblazers in speaking out about their own emotional wellbeing and the struggles they have experienced.[9] However, sometimes simply being open with your emotions can be very powerful. For example, acknowledging to a junior colleague that you are scared or nervous before an important court appearance or client meeting demonstrates that it is fine to experience these feelings and opens the door to that colleague opening up about their own wellbeing. It demonstrates that being a successful lawyer doesn't have to involve being emotionless.

It may be that as a manager you don't feel well-equipped to deal with this type of issue. Perhaps you were promoted because of your lawyering skills rather than your "people skills". If this is the case, it is possible to learn and develop interpersonal skills, so it is important to look for relevant training opportunities to assist you with this.

Reflecting on your emotions

One key way in which lawyers can begin to develop emotional competence is to develop their skills as a reflective practitioner. In other words, someone who builds in the time to think back over their day and use that reflection to (where necessary) modify their reactions and responses going forward.

Lawyers tend to be very analytical and great problem-solvers. This means they may focus on moving forward to resolve the next issue, rather than looking back at past events. Alternatively, they may well spend time thinking back over cognitive aspects of their work, such as a complex piece of legal advice or an interesting point of law. However, there may well be less focus on the less tangible emotional aspects of the role. Being a reflective practitioner means pausing before moving forward to extract relevant information to use going forward.

On the other hand, some lawyers – perhaps those who are something of a perfectionist or "over-thinker" – may find themselves falling into patterns of worrying about the same aspect of their day again and again. Being a reflective practitioner isn't about encouraging that kind of unhelpful rumination. Instead, it is about taking forward lessons from what happened in the past to assist you in future.

You can adapt the questions given earlier in this chapter to assist you with your reflection and either reflect on a particular event that occurred or simply think about the working day as a whole, asking:

- What emotions did I experience today?
- Why did I experience those emotions?
- How did I deal with those emotions?

Based on your answers to these, you can then ask yourself further questions, including:

- Was the way I dealt with those emotions appropriate?
- Did it impact on my wellbeing?
- Is there anything I can change if a similar situation arises in future?
- How can I look after my emotional wellbeing better going forward?

Useful techniques to assist in reflection can include:

- Making a brief note of your emotions throughout the day, for example, inputting emojis on your mobile telephone.
- Keeping a journal focusing on the emotions you experience during the working day.
- Building a support network of family and friends who you can use to "debrief" to. This can be difficult because of the need for confidentiality but focusing on the emotional aspects, rather than the specifics of cases, can help with this.

Coping with strong emotions

Often, people will seek to cope with strong emotions they feel in the workplace using a range of coping mechanisms. Some of these may work in the short-term, but may not be healthy long-term strategies. Internationally, there is evidence that a significant proportion of lawyers turn to alcohol or other substances when they struggle to cope in the workplace.[10] Recognizing and reflecting upon your emotional cues and warning signals can help you ensure you make healthy choices when seeking to cope with the emotional demands of legal work. This can include identifying healthy coping strategies, such as making time to socialize, taking part in hobbies such as yoga or sports and discussing some of the issues you are experiencing with supportive colleagues or friends.

A proactive approach

This chapter has emphasized that emotions are important and valuable within legal workplaces. Rather than ignoring emotions, lawyers can focus on developing their emotional competence to enhance their working practices and give themselves a greater insight into their own emotional wellbeing and that of those around them. Taking a proactive approach and upskilling yourself in this area will provide you with tools that will assist in your legal practice and contribute to a healthier and more sustainable legal workplace.

References

1. For discussion on the role of emotions generally see Feldman Barrett, L. (2018) *How Emotions are Made. The Secret Life of the Brain*, London, Macmillan. For discussion on the intersections between law and emotions see the work of Professor Susan Bandes, DePaul University, US.
2. There are a wide range of different models of emotional intelligence and literacy. This chapter draws on the model of emotional intelligence originally proposed by Peter Salovey and John Mayer in Salovey, P. and Mayer, J. D. (1990) "Emotional Intelligence", *Imagination, Cognition and Personality*, 9(3): 185–211. The term "emotional competence" was first applied to lawyers by the US academic Marjorie Silver in Silver, M. (2004) *The Affective Assistance of Counsel: Practicing Law as a Healing Profession*, Durham, Carolina Academic Press.
3. See, for example, https://www.headspace.com
4. For more information on the relationship between nutrition and your mood see the guidance produced by the UK charity MIND at www.mind.org.uk/information-support/tips-for-everyday-living/food-and-mood/about-food-and-mood/. For support and guidance on sleep issues see the guidance produced by the UK charity LawCare at www.lawcare.org.uk/information-and-support/sleep.
5. For a more detailed explanation of these processes see Kahn, M. (2015) "Jurisprudential Countertransference," *Touro Law Review*: 18(3): Article 5. Available at: http://digitalcommons.tourolaw.edu/lawreview/vol18/iss3/5
6. In the UK and Republic of Ireland, the charity LawCare offers free, confidential telephone and web support at www.lawcare.org.uk. In the US, the American Bar Association offers a range of resources on lawyer wellbeing at www.americanbar.org/groups/lawyer_assistance/resources/lawyer_wellness/
7. For a free online course on developing emotional competence and professional resilience visit www.fitforlaw.org.uk
8. See Jones, E., Graffin, N., Samra, R. and Lucassen, M. (2020) *Mental Health and Wellbeing in the Legal Profession*, Bristol, Bristol University Press.
9. See, for example, Martin, R. (2018) *This Too Will Pass: Anxiety in a Professional World*, Newark, Trigger.
10. A key US study on this is Krill, P. R., Johnson, R. and Albert, L. (2016) "The prevalence of substance use and other mental health concerns among American attorneys", *Journal of Addiction Medicine*, 10(1): 46–52.

Chapter 3:
The Mindful Business Charter

By Kate Dodd, diversity and inclusion consultant, Pinsent Masons LLP

A stroll back in time

Are you sitting comfortably? I'd like to take you back two decades...

The date is September 2000 and I have just started my training contract at a large law firm in the north of England. I have settled into my new office (which I have to myself) and got to know my secretary (who I share with one other trainee). She has been at the firm for a long time and is incredibly helpful, showing me where everything is, filling me in on some of the clients I will be working with (who she knows well), and generally putting me at ease. The Partners in my new team all seem nice, some have their office doors closed, some open, some have computers on their desks, and some don't, on the basis that they "can't be doing with technology" / "these things will never catch on..."

My average day is full but enjoyable, supporting a busy team of employment lawyers and leading on some smaller cases of my own. The majority of correspondence comes via letter (which is read by my supervisor before it comes to me) with the occasional fax arriving from insurers and other "modern" clients that we work with. My phone rings regularly, but all calls go via my secretary, who will take messages if I am busy or seem stressed, and deal with certain queries herself. Let's face it; she has much more experience than me! I am getting used to dictating, enjoying the opportunity for reflection that the process of dictating, checking, and amending drafts (often numerous times) allows for.

When I leave work, I close my office door and that is it for the day. I have no work mobile, and I am not expected to work once I have left. We have the Partners' home phone numbers, in case an emergency arises when they have left and we are still working, but I have never had the need to use them.

Back to reality

Cut to 2020. In the space of two decades, the face of the legal workplace has changed to a point where it is almost unrecognizable from the place where my career began.

The vast majority of offices are open plan and the thought of not having a computer (be it a smart phone or laptop) with you at all times, let alone on your desk, is simply preposterous. Not only do we carry these computers round with us, but we are slaves to them, checking regularly to see what has come in during the minutes since we last checked. The majority of correspondence comes in via email, and what a volume we receive! An average day can easily see 200 emails that need to be read, responded to, and filed.

The role of the legal secretary has changed beyond recognition, with most lawyers now undertaking the majority of their own typing and administration. Where the ratio used to be 1:1 or 1:2, most legal PAs now work with a team of at least six fee earners, and no longer undertake the role of first responder or gatekeeper. The explosion of mobile phones has meant that lawyers are instantly available, and expected to be so, pretty much 24/7.

As well as being able to get hold of their legal advisers immediately, clients have come to expect instantaneous advice, usually via phone or email. Tight deadlines can be set in the knowledge and expectation that they will be met. Not only has this development made life more stressful, but that valuable thinking time, the opportunity to draft, amend, and review, has simply disappeared.

As well as expectations of quicker turnaround times and 24/7 availability, lawyers staying connected while on holiday, joining conference calls during family time, and working outside of core hours has become commonplace. For some, it is even seen as a badge of honor. But with all of this availability and reactivity comes a loss of control. Time is no longer one's own, and long-standing commitments have to fall by the wayside at the drop of a hat (or the drop of an email into an inbox). We know that a lack of control is not good for wellbeing, and there is no doubt that these practices as a whole have increased workplace stress, and have led to burnout and mental health issues.

A race to the bottom?

When we talk about the "race to the bottom" we usually think about big corporates cutting corners to undermine their competitors, or discount retailers slashing prices to win market share, but many now suggest that the legal industry is falling into the same trap. The desire to reduce costs in order to win work has led to unprecedented pressure being placed on lawyers. Somehow, the value placed on deep and connected client relationships appears to have been replaced with a value placed on how quickly things can be turned around, and how cheaply.

For many years the effect of these working practices on mental health and wellbeing has not been discussed. The words "mental health" themselves are generally shrouded in taboo in the legal workplace, with mysterious absences and unexplained exits only ever being spoken about in hushed tones. I am not sure when it was that we hit crisis point in the profession, but there is no doubt that we are facing an unprecedented situation that must be addressed. A number of individuals and organizations have been speaking about this for many years (some of whom are also contributors to this book), but what occurred to us back in 2017 was that the time had come for the *majority* to act.

A meeting at Canary Wharf

Similar to a number of major UK law firms, Pinsent Masons has long enjoyed a strong working relationship with Barclays. In the summer of 2017, usual client/panel firm discussions around mental health and well-being took a turn for the unusual. Like us, Barclays had been working at addressing the effects of stress at work, and reducing stigma around mental health and, like us, had been doing so with significant success. Numerous conversations on these topics had taken place, along with plans for joint initiatives and speaker events etc.

On this particular day in the summer of 2017, we met with Barclays alongside fellow panel firm, Addleshaw Goddard. From the usual initial conversations, a new one sprang up. Rather than looking at the effects, we asked ourselves what we were doing to change the working practices that were so harmful to wellbeing? We asked ourselves whether, rather than dealing with the fall out, could we change the way in which we work so they don't happen in the first place? We agreed that, together, we could. And with that, the spark that was to turn into the Mindful Business Charter was ignited.

Before we left the room, we agreed five key things between us:

- Firstly, that we would work collaboratively, and that although Pinsent Masons and Addleshaw Goddard are traditionally competitors, there would be no element of competition in our efforts to find an industry-wide solution.

- Secondly, Barclays agreed that they would come on board to bring the client perspective, recognizing that as clients are often at the root of private-practice wellbeing challenges, they were uniquely able to help us to address them. They also agreed that they would bring their significant buying power to bear in order to bring other firms on board.
- Thirdly, it was agreed that this initiative would be open to all. From the large to the small, private practice or in-house, anyone working in professional service or corporate industries would be able to participate. The only barrier to entry would be that organizations would need to have *board-level* commitment to sign up. We recognized that this work would not be easy, and therefore knew that anything less than commitment from the very top would be a serious challenge to implementation.
- Fourthly, although it was fantastic to have such senior involvement in the shape of Phillip Aitken and David McCahon (Barclays), Richard Foley (senior partner, Pinsent Masons) and Charles Penney (senior partner, Addleshaw Goddard), it was agreed that we would immediately engage with those working "at the coal face" to ensure that we were able to reflect the everyday realities of legal practice.
- Finally, we acknowledged that this was not going to be easy, but that nothing that matters ever is. We knew that we would face the doubters and the haters, but that if we didn't try then we would never achieve.

A journey of a thousand miles begins with a single step

So, the idea had been born. What on earth to do next?! I resisted the urge to lie down in a darkened room, and, along with Mary Peterson and her team at Addleshaw Goddard, and the team at Barclays, we got to work.

Figure 1 sets out the steps we took, and what is yet to come, with fuller details below.

Our first step was to draw upon the wealth of intellectual capital and perspectives within our businesses, bringing together lawyers, D&I and talent specialists, and client relationship management teams. We wanted to ensure that we looked at the initiative from every angle, so that it was not seen as being workable internally but not externally, or workable for lawyers but not for business operations teams within law firms etc.

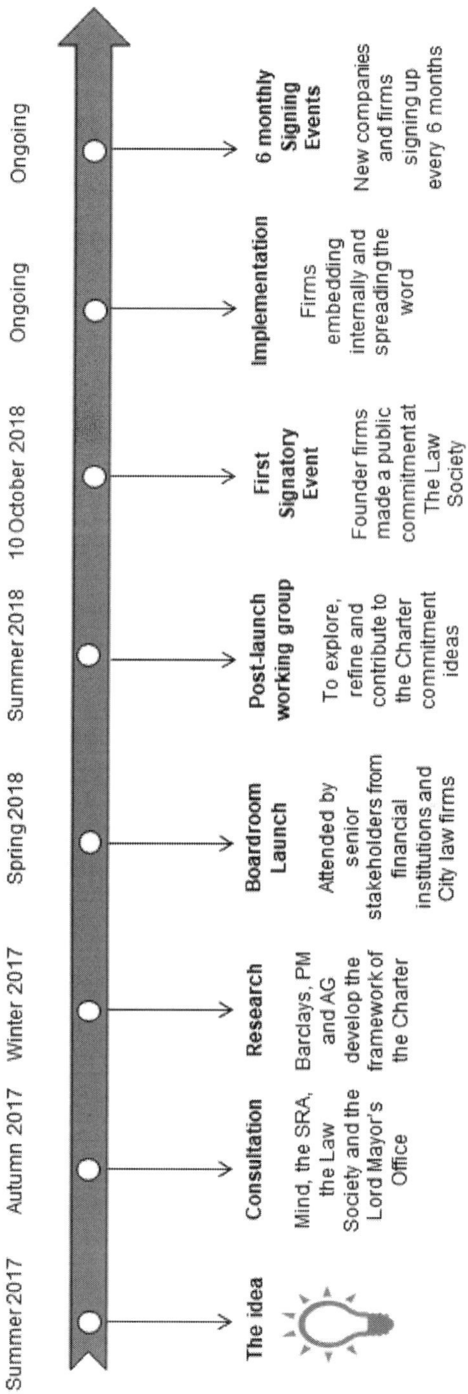

Figure 1: Mindful Business Charter progress and goals.

Working together, we produced a report that examined the relationship between financial institutions and their law firms and uncovered some of the key challenges that are traditionally considered "part and parcel" of working in the legal profession. We looked at which of these could perhaps be alleviated if behaviors were modified, and came up with a list of 22 possible "commitments" to correspond.

We also knew that we needed to consult with the relevant charities and organizations over our plans, including mental health charity Mind, LawCare, the Solicitor's Regulatory Authority, the Law Society and the Lord Mayor's Office. We were delighted with their responses, and the fact that they unanimously supported our work.

Having agreed Board-level buy in as a prerequisite to organizational involvement, our next step was to ask a selection of senior leaders and partners from financial institutions and city law firms to attend a Boardroom Launch, hosted by Phil Aiken, Richard Foley, and Charles Penney, to socialize the idea that we had been working on. Providing the report in advance, we explained that we were seeking high level commitment to develop with us a set of best practice working commitments that promote wellbeing across the sector. We explained that the ultimate goal was to agree between us an impactful charter that would set out simple strategies and ways of working that could potentially make a real difference to the mental health and wellbeing of our people. The Boardroom Launch was a great success. Attendees discussed growing issues with retention, sickness absence, engagement levels and recruitment. We discussed that whilst we don't employ bad people, we all employ people who exhibit bad behaviors from time to time, particularly when under stress. We agreed that if we wished to maintain the legal profession as an attractive place to work for the next generation, it was essential that we act now.

The next step was to host a collaborative workshop to test and challenge the 22 draft commitments created. We invited each organization to nominate three people (of different levels of seniority) working "at the coal face" to attend. We definitely felt some slight trepidation when inviting 40 lawyers into a room to debate a sensitive topic (!) but the whole process was incredibly successful, with very clear themes and the crunch points around wellbeing emerging.

The Mindful Business Charter is born

Based on all of the feedback generated, we created a set of principles that we christened the Mindful Business Charter, which were flexible enough to be deployed across a wide range of professional and financial services. The full Charter is set out overleaf. Whilst individually the commitments listed may sound like small behavioral changes, together they hold the potential to substantially reduce unnecessary stress in the workplace, which is the ultimate goal of the Charter.

Ultimately, as a group, we recognized that we cannot remove *all* sources of stress, but taking steps to remove the avoidable ones will result in people feeling happier, valued and more positive about their careers. We also recognized that continued interruptions have a significant impact on how we feel about our jobs, our relationships, and family life.

Importantly, we were keen to ensure measurability so it was agreed that performance against the Charter's principles would be measured at all law firm / client relationship review meetings, with parties being prompted (possibly for the first time!) to give honest feedback in both directions. Signatories were also required to mark themselves for compliance against the Charter commitments at the end of all significant transactions or projects. We were aware that, without these inbuilt checks and balances, compliance with the Charter may well become nothing more than lip service.

At the same time as finalizing the commitments, we were busy working on an implementation toolkit so that, alongside the Charter itself, we could provide signatories with the practical tools they would need for adoption.

The first signing

Having agreed the Charter principles, it was time to sign! We reached out to our networks and invited all interested parties to participate.

The signing event took place on World Mental Health Awareness Day – 10 October 2018 – at the Law Society in London. In addition to the three founding organizations, Lloyds Banking Group (LBG), RBS, and law firms Ashurst, Baker McKenzie, Clifford Chance, Eversheds Sutherland, Hogan Lovells, Norton Rose Fulbright, and Simmons & Simmons all signed up. In a packed room, the global heads of these organizations each came forward to symbolically sign a copy of the Charter. There have been few moments in my career when I have felt so proud, inspired, and excited for the future.

Mindful Business Charter

The intention of the **Mindful Business Charter** is to remove unnecessary sources of workplace stress and promote better mental health and wellbeing in the legal community. We recognise that there will be times and transactions when long-hours and stress cannot be avoided, but this isn't always the case, and we want it to become the exception rather than the rule. In this way, the Charter is brave and commercial. It recognises that we cannot remove all sources of stress, nor will change happen overnight – but as a legal community we have a responsibility to try do things differently.

MY ORGANISATION'S COMMITMENT

- Drive forward the actions and change necessary to support the Mindful Business Charter.
- Promote a culture where people can speak up early about any concerns that they might have with their wellbeing (or the wellbeing of colleagues).
- Make performance against the Mindful Business Charter / responsible business a priority standing agenda item for all relationship review meetings.
- Ensure responsible business is included as an area of assessment during significant procurement processes.
- Once established, introduce the Mindful Business Charter to one new member every 12 months.

MY COMMITMENT

Openness and respect

BUILDING TRUST AND EFFECTIVE COMMUNICATION:

- Discussing upfront with my colleagues, clients and contacts their preferred method of communication and clarifying any relevant implications of an individual's working patterns.
- Treating internal colleagues and external contacts with the appropriate level of respect and courtesy.
- Asking for and providing feedback to others on a regular basis.

Smart meetings and emails

ADHERING TO SMART MEETING AND EMAIL GUIDANCE:

- Allowing people to join meetings by the method they deem suitable, providing dial in details as default on meeting invites unless it is imperative that everyone attends in person.
- Being respectful of others' time by planning meetings properly (considering who needs to attend / giving appropriate notice / setting clear agendas and objectives) and avoiding last minute cancellations.
- Avoiding over-use of email and not copying people into emails that they don't need to receive.
- Making use of subject lines in emails and ensuring these are reflective of the email's content.

Respecting rest periods

CONSIDERATION GIVEN TO THE NEED TO 'SWITCH OFF':

- Where support is required outside of someone's core working hours, giving them options for when that could be (early morning or evening / weekend).
- When sending emails outside of business hours, being clear in the title whether it needs to be read / actioned promptly or considering sending pre-timed emails (so emails are not received late at night and at weekends).
- Including working hours / availability as part of my email signature, so people are aware of each others' working patterns.
- Respecting people's right to take annual leave without the expectation of them checking emails / being on call, and role modelling the same behavior myself where possible.

Mindful delegation

IMPLEMENTING A BEST PRACTICE APPROACH TO COLLABORATION, INSTRUCTION AND DELEGATION:

- Respecting the need to provide sufficient context and information for a piece of work, ideally including the purpose and ultimate recipient.
- When instructing on a task, negotiating rather than imposing a deadline, being transparent where possible on the wider timetable, and promptly communicating timing changes which impact others.
- When being instructed on a task, being confident to flag when a deadline is unrealistic and / or unachievable.

be brave.

Figure 2: Charter commitments.

What next?

Having reached the milestone of the first signing, the founding 12 set out to launch the Charter within our own businesses.

At Pinsent Masons, rather than going all-firm from day one, we decided to start the implementation in our UK banking and restructuring team, given these were the people working with Barclays, LBG, and RBS on a day-to-day basis. We also felt that starting with a group of hundreds, rather than thousands, would allow us to trial and test methods of implementation in a controlled manner. We set up a Mindful Business Charter Working Group made up of banking and restructuring lawyers of different levels and geographical locations, and other professionals from across our responsible business, D&I and business development teams, and got to work!

A few months in, feedback from the banking and restructuring team (principally the partners and supervisors) was that, although they understood and agreed with the Charter principles, they would appreciate some practical examples of how they worked day-to-day. Following consultation with the teams, the Code of Conduct was born, which acts as a guiding light in the relationship between supervisors and those they work with (be they partners, fee-earners, or PAs).

To mark the launch of the Code of Conduct we held a panel event in July 2019. The event was an opportunity to build interest, answer questions, and gather feedback on areas to focus upon. We were delighted to

Mindful Business Charter

CODE OF CONDUCT

MY COMMITMENT

Openness and respect

Be available to your team

- Increase the use of alternative forms of communication (such as jabber) to give quick updates on jobs, check for capacity and acknowledge emails etc.

Be a mentor

- If capacity allows, invite junior lawyers to join meetings to observe and learn.
- Ensure feedback and corrections are timely, constructive and delivered within the correct environment. Debrief after transactions to allow for continuous learning.

Be fair and inclusive

- Be mindful that junior lawyers and trainees are still learning - they will make mistakes and do things differently but they must be given the time to learn.
- Ensure junior lawyers are kept up to date and copied in to relevant correspondence to allow them to stay fully informed.

Give due credit

- Allow team members to take credit and say thank you for a job well done.

Respecting rest periods

Actively consider wellbeing

- Recognise the need to switch-off and the danger of being 'always on'.

Respect evenings and weekends

- Whilst recognising that everyone likes to work differently, consider the impact of emails sent late at night / over the weekend. Make use of delayed delivery where possible.

Be mindful of non-working days & discourage presenteesim

- Respect the 'out of office', including your own. Role model behaviour by only replying or forwarding emails in critical circumstances.
- Encourage people to be open about non-working days/times.
- Allow people time to catch up on emails when they return to the office after a non-working day or annual leave.
- Be mindful of those not working full time; have a conversation before deciding whether a piece of work can be allocated to them

Smart meetings and emails

Be flexible and considerate

- Consider peoples' working patterns when planning meetings. Be conscious of the additional strain that breakfast/early evening meetings can place on people (with or without families).
- Be open to team members' having a 'non-negotiable' (i.e. the one thing they don't want to miss, whether this be children's bed time, or a gym class).

Don't assume availability

- Review which team members need to be on each call and try to stick to the scheduled times to allow people to plan their day accordingly.

Encourage agility

- Consciously take advantage of agile working - ensure seating allows for a mix of senior and junior people and integrates all of the team. Share learning with more junior members of the team, including across different locations.

Give reasonable notice

- Allow time for team members to respond to emails, if an immediate response is needed, mark as urgent.

Mindful delegation

Challenge your team, but don't overwhelm them

- Check capacity of the team before organising a meeting and in advance of a client call to ensure visibility of deadlines.
- If working remotely, or in different offices, acknowledge emails in context of response time to the client.

Allocate work equally and fairly

- Brief work in plenty of time, ensure that work is allocated appropriately to deadlines.
- Work closely as a team throughout deals and discuss capacity to ensure work is shared evenly.

Find teachable moments

- Take time to brief work or explain mark ups rather than leaving it on someone's chair.

Don't set or accept fake deadlines

- Communicate internal deadlines clearly so junior lawyers can factor in review times for senior team members. Avoid setting 'fake' internal deadlines.

Challenge unreasonable clients

- Be brave - question the clients' rationale for the timing of instructions to gain a proper understanding of the urgency. Manage expectations and negotiate when a client request is unreasonable or unrealistic.

be brave.

Figure 3: Code of Conduct.

hear anecdotal feedback on the impact of the Mindful Business Charter, including the fact that the phrase "that's not very MBC" has come into common usage! We also followed up on the Code of Conduct launch with a series of "Speak Your Mind" sessions, at which our people are encouraged, in a confidential forum, to discuss their thoughts about the Charter and the Code, and to highlight any behaviors or issues that are challenging its implementation.

As well as our UK banking and restructuring teams, our entire Singapore, Hong Kong, and Middle Eastern offices have adopted the Charter. In addition to personal implementation, our teams in those offices are working hard and collaborating with others locally in order to embed the Charter in their regions. Our Australian and Irish offices are adopting the Charter shortly. 1 May 2020 will mark a significant milestone for us, with the launch of the Charter across the rest of our UK offices and teams. Externally, the founding signatories continued to spread the word and bring new organizations into the fold, and it quickly became apparent that we would need some expert support to help us grow and embed the Charter across the legal industry. Cue the arrival of the inspirational Richard Martin and his fantastic team at byrne·dean. Appointed in early 2019, they have worked tirelessly to grow, support, and strengthen the Charter, and under their stewardship we have held another two signing events and the Charter has been adopted by more than 40 organizations across the financial services, legal, and commercial sectors. We are also able to spread the word about the Charter via our informative website – www.mindfulbusinesscharter.com

We have our next signing event in May 2020, and will hold an event every six months to welcome new signatories. Our law firm signatories are working hard to bring their clients on board, and the corporate and financial services signatories are doing the same with their panel firms. Together, we will keep pressing ahead until the Charter is adopted across our industry.

So, what has actually changed?

Improving mental health and wellbeing will not happen overnight – it is a program that will take sustained effort over a number of years. However, within Pinsent Masons, this initiative has already been impactful in getting teams to accept that we can do things differently and, when we do, service quality and delivery improve. It has also sent a clear message that the topic of wellbeing and mental health is not taboo.

We formally introduced the Mindful Business Charter to Pinsent Masons in October 2018. We decided, before launch, to take the temperature with a brief set of questions that we would be able to repeat every three months to assess progress. Using the data generated, we have found that between its inception and March 2020, within UK banking, a number of pulse survey respondents agreed or strongly agreed:

- *"that they are treated with respect and integrity"* increased by three percent to 96 percent;
- *"that they can work flexibly"* increased by 19 percent to 93 percent;
- *"that their time is adequately respected when organizing meetings or calls"* increased by 11 percent to 85 percent;
- *"that their annual leave/non-working days are respected by others"* increased by 11 percent to 95 percent; and
- *"that they feel they can adequately communicate concerns re timescales / deadlines"* increased by five percent to 77 percent.

Feedback gathered from the Speak Your Mind sessions has included:

- "I have seen a big shift in our team culture since I came back from a recent period of leave. The MBC was adopted during my leave and the working atmosphere is more open now. We are trusted to work from home."
- "We are still very responsive to client needs, but senior people seem much more willing to talk to clients to assess if deadlines are really necessary."
- "People are using Jabber (instant messaging) and alternative forms of communication much more. We have fewer face-to-face meetings just for the sake of it now."
- "I have just been off on holiday for two weeks and noticed a remarkable reduction in email traffic. As a result of the MBC, people are thinking about who emails are going to and my name has been taken off the email chains."
- "I have noticed an increase in partners trying to lead by example, i.e. trusting people to look after matters in their absence and asking them to text them with questions if on leave, rather constantly checking emails."
- "We are getting better and more respectful of the different pressures people face. We feel more able to talk about what's happening outside of work."

As well as seeing positive changes across the banking and restructuring team, we have also seen a significant reduction in the number of people who are concerned about the possible impact of the Mindful Business Charter on productivity and competitiveness. It is now widely understood that the Mindful Business Charter is not a "snowflake charter". It is not designed to stop people from working long hours, or to create situations in which tight deadlines are not met; rather it is about separating out the truly urgent from the "nice to have". We know that a lack of control over one's own workload and working day is a significant challenge to wellbeing, and the Mindful Business Charter seeks to give back some of the control by facilitating open conversations in which deadlines can be discussed and agreed ways of working can be established. We have also found that discussions around the Mindful Business Charter have led to constructive conversations around team culture. There is no doubt that providing a forum for such discussions to take place has had a positive impact on wellbeing and engagement.

Externally, we have been delighted to have won awards for our work. As well as being shortlisted and highly commended in a number of categories, the three of us who designed the Charter won the Human Resource Innovation Award at the Legal Week Innovation Awards 2019 and Best Innovation in the HR In Law Awards 2019.

Acknowledgements

It is almost impossible to name and thank all of the fantastic people who have helped bring the Mindful Business Charter from idea to the industry-changing initiative it is today, and I will no doubt miss some people out! The Mindful Business Charter is an industry-wide collaboration in its truest sense, and it will not survive without the tireless work that so many people are doing externally, and within their own organizations.

Special commendation has to go to Phil Aiken of Barclays for his spark of an idea, and his vision in bringing panel firms together to work as one. David McCahon, along with the Barclay's Mindful Business Charter team, also deserve a great deal of thanks.

Charles Penney, Mary Peterson and the team at Addleshaw Goddard have been fantastic co-founders and have worked tirelessly to make progress. What a pleasure it has been to collaborate with a firm that shares so many of our own values.

At Pinsent Masons, Richard Foley of course has led from the front on this since day one. Without him, the Charter simply would not exist. I must also thank Steph Powell, who did so much of the organization and supported me with first drafts, ideas, and unwavering enthusiasm in the early days. Thanks also to Jacquie Dunn and her team, and the original Mindful Business Charter Dream Team; Matt Morgan, Rebecca Latus, Stan Verkaik, Alice Burden, Becca Labib, Alvin Ho, Valerie Wu, Catherine Workman, and Sania Khan. A special mention must of course go to the UK banking and restructuring team; both the wonderful Mindful Business Charter Working Group, who have trailblazed and supported us at every turn, and the team itself who have courageously been our guinea pigs and first adopters.

Thanks to Emma Mamo and the team at Mind, to the SRA, the Law Society, Elizabeth Rimmer and the team at LawCare, the Lord Mayor's Office and all of the other likeminded folk out there who are supporting, championing, and endorsing our work.

Thanks to Richard Martin, Matt Dean, and all of the team at byrne·dean who have gone above and beyond (and beyond again) their original remit to make the Charter such a success.

Finally, of course, huge thanks must go to the nine founding signatories who joined the original three, and turned the Mindful Business Charter from an idea into a movement. Thanks also to all of those who have signed up since who will, by the time you are reading this, hopefully be in the hundreds.

Chapter 4:
Culture and practice of law – creating lasting change

By Elizabeth Rimmer, chief executive, LawCare

It's not new

LawCare, the charity that promotes and supports good mental health and wellbeing in the legal community throughout the UK and Ireland, has its origins in the Lawyers Support Group. The Lawyers Support Group, formed in 1983, brought lawyers from all walks of the profession in recovery from alcohol addiction together and met regularly in London.

In 1995, partly prompted by a letter in the *Law Society Gazette*, Charles Elly, president of the Law Society of England and Wales, set up a working party to look into helping members of the profession affected by alcohol misuse. SolCare, as it was then called, was registered as a charity in April 1997 and Barry Pritchard, a solicitor who was a recovering alcoholic with 13 years' sobriety, became the first chief executive. During that first year SolCare took 60 calls from solicitors with alcohol problems. At that time the mental health and wellbeing issues we are now increasingly talking about in the legal community were a hidden secret.

Fast forward to 2020 and SolCare has become LawCare, and our remit has spread to all branches of the legal profession across the UK and Ireland. In 2019 we took nearly 1,000 contacts on our helpline and webchat on a range of issues such as stress, depression, bullying, and alcohol, with over 40,000 visits to our website.

The recent surge in awareness and engagement about mental health across legal education, training and practice has come alongside increasing public awareness of mental health, driven by high profile national campaigns and an increased focus on workplaces' responsibilities to their staff. There is perhaps a perception that this growing recognition is related to the changes in the way we work and the hyper-connected world of the 21st century. Yet LawCare's roots go back to the 1980s, a time when working long hours either meant staying at the office or taking a large briefcase of papers home; communication with clients and colleagues was by letter; we didn't have mobile phones and no one had a PC on their desk. The roots of the mental health issues we see in the legal profession today are not solely based on the 24/7 culture, although these are additional factors now – the roots lie in the culture and practice of law. If we want to find solutions to these issues we need to understand what it is about the culture and practice of law that is having a negative impact and look at what we can do differently to better prepare lawyers for life in the law and support good mental health.

Going back to basics – what is wellbeing?

Wellbeing is subjective and means different things to different people, but it's about how we feel, how we think, our relationships, how we find meaning and purpose in our lives. We each want to live happy and fulfilling lives and wellbeing matters to each of us.

Wellbeing is a fundamental component of the World Health Organization's definition of mental health. WHO defines mental health as "a state of wellbeing in which every individual realizes his or her own potential, can cope with the normal stresses of life, can work productively and fruitfully, and is able to make a contribution to her or his community". At LawCare we use this definition of mental health as it has wellbeing at its heart and it looks at mental health in a positive and holistic way.

About 50 percent of our wellbeing is influenced by our genes, ten percent is related to our upbringing and external circumstances such as our health, work, or financial situation, but crucially about 40 percent is influenced by our choices and attitudes – how we approach relationships, our values, and our sense of purpose.

This means we can take positive steps to influence our wellbeing. There has been considerable research into the science of wellbeing and new evidence about the factors that affect it. This gives us an opportunity to use this evidence to make better choices and increase our wellbeing in our personal lives, homes, schools, workplaces, and communities.

Evidence suggests that there are five steps we can each take to improve our wellbeing:

1. Connect – with the people around you, your family, friends, colleagues and neighbors. it's important to spend time developing these relationships;
2. Be active – finding an activity that you enjoy and make it part of your life;

3. Keep learning – learning new skills can boost confidence;
4. Give to others – even small acts such as a kind word or a thank you count; and
5. Be mindful – be more aware of the present moment, including your feelings and thoughts, your body and the world around you. "Mindfulness" can positively change the way you feel about life and how you approach challenges.

It's important to keep in mind that the steps to positive wellbeing are relatively simple; the hard part is committing to them and making the time for them. When we are under pressure at work or experiencing a busy spell, we prioritize doing more work, overlooking our wellbeing, so rather than making time for family, friends, exercise or eating well, we compromise those so we can spend more time working, in the belief that working longer is the key to being more productive. In actual fact, prioritizing time for the activities that support our wellbeing will make us more productive and better able to manage the pressure of work.

Why does mental health matter in the professional context?

Mental health in the law matters on three levels – individual, workplace, and the wider legal community.

Individual

Wellbeing at an individual level doesn't just matter because of the benefits it brings – such as greater self-esteem, optimism, self-determination, resilience and positive relationships with colleagues – it also matters as it's fundamental to being a good lawyer.

Practicing law is a high stakes job; lawyers have to pass tough exams and progress through rigorous training to qualify; legal professionals are regulated and held to high standards of honesty and integrity. Clients depend on the skill and knowledge of legal professionals to provide reliable advice and resolve problems, and they expect their lawyer to be competent and trustworthy. Legal work requires clarity of mind and focus.

Lawyers who are sleep deprived, regularly work long hours, feel overwhelmed by their case load and pressured to meet their billing target or the expectation of clients, are more likely to make mistakes or poor ethical decisions. Stress contributes to raised levels of cortisol and other hormones that negatively affect the brain's ability to function and process information. Lawyers experiencing stress, anxiety, or depression can find it difficult to concentrate, pay attention to detail, or interact with colleagues, and have their judgement and decision-making skills compromised. They are less likely to meet the high standards expected of them by both their clients and regulators. Recognizing and learning how to manage the signs and triggers of poor mental health are important to achieving positive legal wellbeing.

There have been recent cases of solicitors in England and Wales who have been struck off by the Solicitors Regulation Authority for breaching codes of professional misconduct when they were experiencing poor mental health (see chapter ten). In the first instance when these cases were heard before the Tribunal, the solicitors were found to be dishonest but were not struck off, as there was recognition that they were experiencing mental health problems. However, on appeal to the High Court by the regulator, the High Court ruled that the pressure of work or extreme working conditions "cannot either alone or in conjunction with stress or depression" justify not striking off dishonest solicitors. These solicitors made poor decisions that cost them their legal careers. Had these lawyers worked in environments where they felt supported and psychologically safe, they may have been able to share the problems they were experiencing and get support before it was too late.

Workplace

As a lawyer your mind is your greatest asset and looking after it must be a priority, both for you and your employer/legal workplace.

From an organization's perspective, actively committing to improving and supporting good wellbeing and mental health creates workplaces where people thrive, where people want to come to work and do their best. Benefits to organizations that embed mental health across the workplace and promote a culture of acceptance include:

- Attracting a talented and diverse range of employees;
- Improved retention of valued and experienced staff;
- Reduction in sick absence;
- Increased productivity;
- Competitive advantage; and
- Better morale and a positive workplace culture.

The wider legal community

Good mental health in the legal community helps to maintain the reputation of the legal profession and advance the administration of justice.

Coverage about lawyer mental health is no longer confined to the legal media; these stories are now being covered by the national UK media such as the BBC, *The Guardian*, *The Times*, and the *Financial Times*.

The public perhaps don't always recognize the value the legal community provides as a bedrock for upholding civil society and the rights many take for granted – the work done to ensure the most vulnerable in society have access to justice or hold authorities such as government and public services to account for their decisions. The public place their trust and confidence in the legal profession every day to deliver effective legal services – from buying a home to selling a business – and poor lawyer mental health could undermine this.

The legal environment

The legal landscape is changing. Economic realities, new technologies and ways of working alongside client pressures are colliding with different expectations and working styles of younger lawyers. Many clients no longer want to pay for legal services in the traditional way, leading to more fixed fees and consultancy-style law firms. Many lawyers no long want to work in a "traditional firm" and financial rewards for very long hours are less appealing. Law firms and legal workplaces need to keep pace with these changes if they are to recruit and retain the best talent and remain viable longer term.

The thinking styles of lawyers can also contribute to poor mental health. Legal work requires prudence – lawyers have to be careful and considered, look for potential problems and link these to the worst case scenario; they often have to think pessimistically. Lawyers strive for perfection and often have a fixed mindset that everything they do has to be perfect, there is a fear of failure or making a mistake, and lawyers see their role as resolving other people's problems without recognizing that they may have some of their own. A very common thinking style is rumination – the tendency to repetitively think about the causes, factors, and consequences of negative emotional experiences, replaying scenarios over and over in their head.

Combine these thinking styles with –

- long working hours that can lead to social isolation;
- pressure to meet billing targets;
- the 24/7 culture and always being "on";
- the stigma of admitting you are feeling overwhelmed or have a mental health issue;

- managing the expectations of clients;
- working with vulnerable people;
- the lack of support or even time for management responsibilities;
- the forced cultural norms that can lead to exclusion;
- presenteeism; and
- no vocabulary to talk about emotions and how the work affects you

– and you create a perfect storm for the stress, anxiety and depression we see in the legal profession. There are high levels of negative emotions within law as the work is often about winning or losing and can require lawyers to be critical, judgmental, combative, and aggressive.

Emotional competence – fit for law

Some think there is no place for emotion in the law and believe emotions interfere with rational thinking. Law students are trained to "think like a lawyer", suppressing and ignoring their emotions, which is not beneficial to wellbeing. In fact, there is a huge body of scientific evidence that proves cognition and emotion are intertwined. If we consider that emotions affect our actions, decision-making, reasoning, thought processes and judgement, we can clearly see the relevance of emotion in the law.

Lawyers often enter the workplace without the emotional competencies needed to meet the demands of an evolving profession. Emotional competency is about how we understand and handle our emotions as well as identifying and interpreting emotional responses around us. These skills, often known as "soft skills", are not traditionally valued or developed within legal education and training, which is focused on developing the ability to think, reason, and analyze.

Providing legal professionals with resources to enable them to understand and develop key emotional competencies such as emotional self-awareness, self-reflection, and better strategies for emotional self-regulation is one way in which to equip them more effectively for practice, enhance their wellbeing, and potentially reduce levels of stress, anxiety, and depression.

LawCare wants to encourage legal professionals to proactively recognize and identify factors that put a strain on their wellbeing at an early stage, rather than responding retrospectively once issues with mental health and wellbeing have arisen. We know from our work in supporting lawyers for over two decades how difficult it is for lawyers to admit they are struggling with the pressures of work, which often leads them to seek help when they are nearing crisis.

The Open University and the University of Sheffield, in collaboration with LawCare, has developed an interactive learning resource called "Fit for Law". The course aims to provide legal professionals with key skills in emotional competence and professional resilience to enhance their wellbeing and enable them to be their best at work.

The first module, "Managing and Understanding Yourself", focuses on managing and understanding emotions and stress and developing healthy working practices. It includes videos and activities and takes under four hours to complete or can be broken down into bite-size chunks. Fit for Law is evidence-based and relevant to all who work in the law and is free to access at www.fitforlaw.org.uk.

About LawCare – our vision

LawCare is an independent charity offering emotional support, information, and training to the legal community in the UK and Ireland. We work to promote good mental health and wellbeing in legal workplaces and drive change in education, training, and practice. We've listened to thousands of legal professionals and no one knows lawyers like we do.

Our emotional support service offers a safe place to talk without judgement. We're here to help, with helpline calls, emails, and webchats answered in confidence by trained staff and volunteers who have first-hand experience of working in the law. We also have a network of peer supporters. We also support legal workplaces – organizations can turn to us for resources and training on how to create mentally healthy workplaces.

We help all branches of the legal profession and our support spans the legal life from student to training to practice and retirement. Whether you're a barrister feeling burnt out, a young trainee experiencing sexual harassment, a student struggling with workload, support staff worrying about a mistake you've made, a senior lawyer feeling like you're being pushed out – we're here to listen.

In 2019 we had nearly 1,000 people turn to us for support with the most common reasons being stress, bullying and harassment, and depression. We have seen a significant increase in contacts related to bullying and harassment, with these contacts nearly doubling in both 2018 and 2019, aligned with the #metoo movement and a growing awareness that behaviors that were once tolerated or ignored are no longer acceptable.

There is a shared interest across the legal professions and providers of legal education in each jurisdiction we serve to promote and support better mental health and wellbeing. LawCare is the organization that bridges all the legal professions and jurisdictions in the UK and Ireland so is well placed to influence greater collaboration to better understand and address the culture and practice of law that is contributing to poor mental health and wellbeing. We want to lead the way in bringing the community together to address these common concerns and identify how we can create lasting change in the way we educate and train lawyers and support them in practice.

Culture change – steps we can take now

At LawCare we want to motivate everyone in the legal community to take positive action about mental health – individuals, workplaces, regulators, educators, and professional bodies. These are the steps that can be taken now to lead to lasting change:

Leadership

We believe that to really change the culture in an organization, leaders have to be on board and drive the change. Leaders can demonstrate the organization's commitment to staff wellbeing through their actions – treating colleagues with respect, taking lunch breaks, working healthy hours, talking freely about the stresses and strains of working in the law, and having an open-door policy.

Put wellbeing at the heart of the organization

In order for mental health and wellbeing to be taken seriously it can't be bolted on to an existing business strategy – it needs to be at the very heart of the strategy. One of the key metrics that an organization is measuring should be, how happy are the staff? What could be done to improve their wellbeing? What makes a difference to their lives? Organizations could make staff wellbeing an objective and report on this to the board or senior management committee in the same way they would report on finances, and sharing progress internally and externally would send a clear message that mental health is taken seriously. Happier staff perform better, are less likely to make mistakes, and are less likely to leave their job.

Change target structure

Most lawyers work in an organization where the more hours they work, the better. This is not conducive to good wellbeing. People need time to relax, exercise, see friends and family, and sleep. Without these needs being met, wellbeing deteriorates very quickly and with it judgement, decision-making, and cognitive function. We would like to see legal organizations develop different metrics for measuring success. Moving to an overall project fee rather than billable hours model, for example, or using client satisfaction as a benchmark.

Collaborate with clients and other legal colleagues

Many clients are changing what they want from a law firm, and want to see that firms have considered the mental health and wellbeing of the lawyers working for them. A lot can be achieved through proper, honest conversations about deliverables and timelines – it's not always possible but negotiating on these can make a real difference to the wellbeing of the lawyers working on the case. This equally applies to relationships with other lawyers outside the firm or with counsel.

Training, mentoring, and supervision

Research suggests that the single biggest factor affecting people's wellbeing at work is their boss. Many managers have had no training in how to look after their team, how to talk to colleagues about mental health, what signs of poor mental health to look out for, and how to properly supervise and encourage employees. Good supervision is essential to wellbeing, and people thrive when they are fully supported at work.

Adopt healthy working practices

Legal organizations need to adopt healthy working practices that support wellbeing. For example, an organization-wide policy on not sending work emails outside of core hours, monitoring which staff are not taking breaks or holidays or always staying late, allowing working from home or flexible working hours where possible, and encouraging people to be respectful in the workplace all help.

Challenge stigma

Stigma silences people in the workplace to speak up about mental health. Lawyers find it hard to admit they are struggling or to ask for help for fear of being perceived as weak or not good enough. Some fear it will be a career limiting step. We need to challenge this, so that anyone in need of support feels able to seek it. We need everyone in the legal community speaking up about mental health, sharing their experiences (if they want to) and putting it on the agenda in their workplace.

Legal education

We need to look at how we can embed positive messages about wellbeing into legal education that better prepares students for the transition into practice. This should be a compulsory part of the curriculum, not an optional extra.

Regulation

Regulators should step up their engagement about mental health in the legal profession and move beyond raising awareness of the problems to developing their role in being part of the solution. The legal profession depends on trust and if lawyers do not act with integrity, this can damage public confidence in the legal system. Regulators should give consideration as to how they can support a legal culture that encourages integrity and what steps they can take to sanction legal workplaces that have a poor culture.

The time is now

At LawCare we feel that many are now aware of the scale of the problem facing the legal profession. We know that lawyers are stressed, depressed, and anxious – there are numerous surveys and research that support this along with our own data from the helpline calls, emails, and webchats we receive. We know that lawyers are amongst the most stressed people in the workforce. We know that lawyers work long hours and have little time for anything but work. The big question remains unanswered – what are we all going to do about it? Whilst it is fantastic that more organizations are more switched on to mental health, and that many individuals are taking better care of themselves with regards to exercise, sleep, practicing mindfulness, or spending more time with their friends and family, this will not fix the problems that lie at the very heart of the legal profession.

As a community, we need to come together and seize the current momentum around mental health and start changing the way we work and educate lawyers, so that the law continues to attract a diverse range of talented people and where lawyers thrive rather than just survive.

Chapter 5: Conversations that matter

By Lubna Gem Arielle

What do you do if you are concerned about a colleague's mental health? We may sense that we should say something. Although we know this is important, it's also difficult, and there can be a tendency to delay or avoid taking action.

It's vital that we normalize these conversations and the idea that it's ok to be mentally unwell, in the same way that it's ok to have a physical illness, to discuss it, and ask for help.

Drawing on my work as a corporate facilitator/applied theatre practitioner in having difficult conversations, I designed the NILE model as a framework of support for initiating a conversation with a colleague when you are concerned. The name reflects the flow of life through the desert.

In this chapter, I will give a brief introduction to mental health and highlight a couple of common myths and then explain the model and how to use it, sharing insights from training sessions and my personal journey.

This is a guide to supporting others in the workplace, about first steps that one can take with co-workers. If someone does need help, you would assist in finding this from someone with the appropriate resources, experience, or training.

NILE – a model for conversations that matter

In summary, the four parts of the model are:

- Notice – What changes have you observed?
- Initiate – Know what to say and manage your state so you can say it.
- Listen – Be aware of default modes of listening and what is useful in this context.
- Explore – What options does the other person have (remembering that you are not the expert)?

The challenge

At times, we may be concerned about someone else's mental health, but, all too often, we don't ask. This may result from the stigma that still exists, the silence this all too often engenders in those who are unwell, or the lack of widespread literacy around mental health.

At the same time, the vernacular around fostering a culture of well-being inevitably includes an open, supportive culture on the wish list.

In the UK, the six mental health core standards recommended in *Thriving at Work, the Stephenson/Farmer review of mental health and employers*[1] include encouraging open conversations about mental health and the support available when employees are struggling. Yet, how many of us feel equipped to having these conversations? How far can we rely on someone who is unwell to disclose ill health of their own volition? Are these conversations taking place?

A hesitation to have a conversation exists on both sides. In their work on having conversations about mental health, the Australian organization *Beyond Blue*[2] identified a reluctance on both sides of the equation. Those who are concerned about others have a "low initiation of conversations". Those who are unwell have an "inhibited level of disclosure".

In training sessions, the barriers typically identified include fears about unwanted interference, offending or embarrassing someone, assuming they may not want anyone to know, compromising a working relationship, or looking foolish if one is wrong and not knowing how to respond. There are also concerns around being drawn in and getting too involved or having to take on someone else's workload.

For these or other reasons, we may decide not to say anything. We perhaps assume that the other person will simply tell us if something is wrong or that they will ask for our help if they need it; but these assumptions are flawed and these conversations do matter. From personal experience, they can be the brakes on a slippery slope.

My story

At the end of 2011, I started to experience problems with the new owners in the maisonette beneath me, who started to gut their flat without notifying me. The noise of demolition and subsequent building work with accompanying acrid dust went on for months, and they refused to acknowledge the impact of our shared freehold or the disruption they were causing me. My GP prescribed me with steroids so I could breathe and anti-depressants to help me cope, but the problems escalated.

The stigma around mental health issues made it difficult to talk about how I felt and I was ashamed of being on medication because of my inability to simply deal with my neighbors. Almost a year later, the building works and stonewalling were still ongoing, my medication had been increased but my emotions had spiraled out of control. I was crying for most of my waking hours and my thoughts were dark and dangerous to the extent that I was contemplating suicide.

Fortunately my brother called and stepped in. In hindsight, his actions followed the steps of NILE: he ***noticed*** *something was wrong, took the* ***initiative*** *in asking if I was ok,* ***listened*** *to my response, and* ***explored*** *what I could do next.*

I was placed in the hands of experts and remained under psychiatric supervision and on medication until the end of 2015. For most of this time I appeared relatively "normal" to the outside world. Behind the scenes, I was still recovering from the experience and attempting to reactivate lost parts of myself and my life. I rarely spoke about how I really was.

I had experienced depression in my teens and again in my 30s, but had had a clear run for over a decade. This time round had been the most severe and debilitating.

Background to the NILE model

I came off my medication and still had full recovery ahead of me; I wanted to get my life back on track, of course. I also wanted to understand what had happened. I wanted to extract something meaningful and useful from experiencing what is colloquially described as a total breakdown. I think of it as picking up the broken pieces of myself and turning them into a kaleidoscope.

This prompted me to want to learn more about mental health. In addition to independent research, I trained as an executive coach, with an emphasis on neuroscience, positive psychology, and mental health and wellbeing; I also trained as a Mental Health First Aider[3] and undertook basic training in SafeTalk[4] – how to have a conversation with someone who is suicidal. I started speaking in public about my experience and the lessons learned, and delivered mental health awareness sessions. In response to the conversational gap that I observed, read about, and discussed with contemporaries, I collaborated with leading computer scientists at Trinity College Dublin as the writer and creative director of a Virtual Reality work, "Bridging the Blue",[5] which explores empathic responses to depression and developed the NILE model to use in training sessions.

"We all have mental health"

This expression has become widespread and it is essential to set aside any notions that mental health only equates to mental ill health. Just as with physical health, our mental health moves across a spectrum between being well and unwell, with varying degrees in-between. We might linger at different points on this spectrum at different times, for different durations and some of us may span the entire spectrum while others move within a limited range.

A definition of mental health

The World Health Organization defines mental health as a "state of wellbeing in which every individual realizes his or her own potential, can cope with the normal stresses of life, can work productively and fruitfully and is able to make a contribution to his or her community".

We might view this definition as having four indices and reflect on our own wellbeing in relation to each of them, i.e. how far are we realizing our own potential at work or in our personal lives, coping with the normal stresses of life, working productively or fruitfully or making a contribution to the various communities we are part of.

When assessing our lives across these quite varied questions, we can see that the answer is unlikely to be static and so we can see how we move across a spectrum. It is useful to have this social model that views mental health in terms of social and environmental factors, as opposed to the medical model that looks at mental health in terms of diagnostic criteria.

The mental health spectrum and workplace stress

Using workplace stress as an example, we're told that some stress is good for us and that too much stress can eventually kill us. In small amounts, stress can indeed assist us in powering through a presentation or a tough meeting – we can experience stress and remain well. We may perform well at work and enjoy it.

However, if stress levels are sustained, or there isn't a sufficient gap between one stressful situation and the next and we never have time to recover, we can start to become unwell and potentially develop a mental health condition, such as burnout, which in 2019 was recognized by the World Health Organization[6] as an occupational phenomenon. Symptoms of burnout may include exhaustion, feelings of being overwhelmed and disconnection with work.

Stress can also lead to a mental health condition with clinical diagnostic criteria, such as depression and feelings of helplessness and hopelessness.

It's important to be aware that the build-up of stress is only one route to depression. The causes of depression and other mental disorders are varied and complex.

Just as with physical health, we can take preventative steps to safeguard ourselves from becoming unwell, but these steps are not guaranteed to be effective. Illness of all sorts is sometimes unexpected and is no reflection of our mettle, character, or the amount or effectiveness of any self-care practices. It is not necessarily an indicator of our capability or capacity to perform at work.

Common myths

The many myths about mental health feed the stigma and perpetuate the silence that emerges from it. Below are a few prevalent examples.

Infallibility

Most of us will admit to having physical ailments such as colds, sore throats, or broken bones. Although there may be reluctance to talk about serious physical illnesses, this is not as pervasive a societal taboo. With mental health, however, many of us expect ourselves and others to possess Herculean infallibility. It's just not possible to be in excellent health, every day, for the whole of our lives, but there is still pressure to present ourselves at work, and to the world, this way. The reality is that our mental health may waver.

Cheering up

Depression as an illness is all too often conflated with the *emotion* of feeling depressed. Where it is only our emotions, we probably can cheer up with some distraction, perhaps a few beers or a funny movie. Depression as a mental illness is a clinically diagnosed disorder that needs professional treatment.

Dwelling on the past/thinking of oneself

There is a body of misinformation that seems to stem from motivational quotes or social media memes and suggests that depression arises from dwelling on the past or thinking of oneself, and that we can overcome it by doing more for others. When I was ill, someone suggested that I might feel better by helping a niece with some quadratic equations. Apart from my mind being too gridlocked to have coped with that, I don't think algebra is most people's first port of call for cheering up!

There are many other misconceptions about mental illness. We'll talk more about some of these as we look at the model.

NILE – a four-step model for conversations that matter

The model sets out a framework to help you navigate your way through a conversation about mental health.

NOTICE: What do you observe? What changes have you observed?
The first step is noticing that someone may not be ok.

The model doesn't require you to become a clinician and know how to navigate the diagnostic criteria for mental health conditions/disorders. Mental Health First Aiders are trained to spot signs of common disorders such as depression, anxiety, panic attacks, and schizophrenia. Spotting signs can also be complex as the same signs can occur across various conditions.

Something we can all do is notice changes in the colleagues or co-workers we see regularly. Changes in behavior, appearance, or work patterns can alert us that something may be wrong. For example, a calm, efficient colleague may become irritable or less decisive or make mistakes; a well-dressed co-worker may take less care with their appearance; someone may start coming in or leaving later than normal; or you may suspect use of alcohol or drugs.

These and other changes can alert you that something is wrong. Where you know someone reasonably well, you may just have a general sense that something is not quite right, without being able to pinpoint anything in particular.

A change may be a one-off occurrence or have a plausible explanation such as someone who is usually alert may be tired after a late night out. Where changes persist, we should think about action. NHS guidance for many conditions such as depression is to see a GP if symptoms persist for more than two weeks. When we are observing others, we are unlikely to know when the clock started to run so we may wish to have a conversation sooner than this. It won't hurt.

In summary, this step is noticing changes in a co-worker or having a hunch, especially where this is ongoing.

INITIATE: Getting off to a good start
Ensure you are aware of the resources within your workplace such as Mental Health First Aiders, employee assistance programs, occupational health, GPs and more general organizations such as the Samaritans, before you have the conversation. Do some preparation, including finding contact details, so that these can be shared if needed.

There are three components to the Initiate step – choosing the right time and place, managing your state, and knowing what to say.

Choose the right time and place

Find somewhere private where you won't be disturbed or overheard and make sure that you have sufficient time. It's important the other person is clear they have your full time and attention.

Manage your state

As we said earlier, these conversations may be difficult and/or stressful. In stressful situations our brains may go into panic mode, where the amygdala prepares our body for flight, fight, or to freeze. A conversation with a co-worker we are concerned about may feel difficult, but is not a threat, so we want to engage the executive part of our brain, our pre-frontal cortex, which enables us to remain rational and think things through. It can be helpful, for example, to remind ourselves that this is a conversation with someone we are concerned about and that, although it is difficult, we are prepared.

We need to outsmart our brain and manage our state and we can do this by paying attention to our posture and breath.

Posture and our emotions are directly correlated, with each affecting the other. Dutch behavioral scientist, Erik Peper, undertook research in 2004[7] to show how a simple change of posture affects mood. When we sit up straight, we are more likely to have positive and expansive thoughts.

An erect posture also enables us to breathe more efficiently, allowing the ribs to expand upwards and outwards and for our lungs to expand fully. Slow, deep, rhythmic breathing enables us to access the rational part of our brain.

Ancient wisdom practices tell us about the power of the breath. In the yoga tradition, the practice of Pranayama – breathing through alternate nostrils – is said to calm the mind. Recent scientific advances by Mark Krasnow[8] and his team at Stanford University have identified the parts of the brain that connect breathing to our state of mind, with slow, smooth breathing reducing feelings of anxiety and tension, leading to feelings of calm and facilitating the ability to pay attention.

Managing our state is important as it reassures the other person that it is safe to open up.

Know what to say

What we say when we initiate a conversation is crucial. It's important that we are direct as we raise the subject, to ensure that both people are having the same conversation. The following are some suggested phrases as a starting point. You will find your own words and your own approach as you become more experienced.

Do: Be direct	**Don't:** Be indirect
Are you ok? I've noticed ... Are you ok? For example: I've noticed you've been less patient than you usually are recently. Are you ok? I can't pinpoint what it is exactly, but you don't seem yourself. Is everything ok?	Assume they will tell you. Terrible weather today, isn't it? Are you busy at the moment? How is the case/deal you are working on progressing?

The indirect options of assuming someone will tell you, or asking indirectly by talking about workloads or the weather may be easier in the circumstances, but they are unlikely to be effective in initiating a conversation about mental health. When you ask if someone is ok, don't accept the first answer. The reflex may be to say, "Yes, everything is fine" when it isn't. Wait, and give them time to speak more or ask again.

In the UK, the "ask twice" campaign[9] addresses the importance of not merely accepting the first answer given and suggests asking again.

It is best to be direct in any important conversation. Where you just have a sense that something may be wrong, you can say that you can't pinpoint this exactly. This statement can also be useful if what you have noticed is potentially inflammatory and could make the person defensive, such as if you have noticed their standard of personal hygiene has slipped. You could also use this phrase to get started if being direct just feels too awkward for you. It is important to take care of yourself as well.

LISTEN: Listen to the answer and create a space for the other person to feel safe

The quality of our listening has an impact on whether or not others feel safe, listened to, and willing to open up. Poor listening can close someone down. Consider:

- Being distracted – looking at your phone or laptop or over the other person's shoulder. Keep your focus on them, and look away just enough that they don't feel uncomfortable;
- Responding with your own autobiography – relating whatever is said to your own experience or thoughts. Keep the conversation on them;
- Problem-solving – giving solutions and suggestions. The important thing is to listen, not solve;

- Being defensive – contradicting or objecting to anything that is said; and
- Assuming you know what the other person is going to say – this can lead to a misunderstanding of what is actually going on, and to more harm being done than good.

In training sessions, I often use pair work so participants can experience different modes of listening (one talks as the other listens in one of the styles) and how that makes them feel. The forms of listening described above do not encourage someone to open up and feel safe. It is difficult enough to talk about mental ill health.

When I was unwell, I received a lot of undoubtedly well-intended advice, which didn't help and sometimes hurt, such as suggestions to "get fresh air – it always helps me when I'm blue", or insistence that I should seize control over my thought processes, to "stop thinking about myself" or to "stop dwelling on the past", when I wasn't doing either of these things. My mind was at a standstill, ineffective and ricocheting between blank or a cascade of hopelessness.

Misguided remarks, however well-intended, can be counter-productive – they can lead to self-criticism, magnify a sense of inadequacy, and add to the stigma and the silence.

Non-judgmental listening is the most helpful – simply listening to what is said without attempting to jump to a conclusion or find a solution.

Mental Health First Aid includes non-judgmental listening as a skill on their MHFA training and emphasizes the need to be aware of one's own points of reference and experiences that can lead to judgements being made without noticing. This also underlines why making an effort to consistently raise our individual literacy about mental illness can be invaluable.

Listening tips

- Give the other person space to think – don't interrupt; allow pauses.
- Use prompts:
  - "Tell me more."
  - "I'm listening."
  - Encourage with listening noises.

- Watch out for ambiguity – are they congruent, i.e. do body language and tone match what is being said? E.g. saying, "Yes, I'm fine" in a strained voice or in contradictory body language.
- Be aware – what are they not saying?

What if someone insists they are ok?

There are a couple of possibilities. It may be that they are ok! You still did the right thing to check. Or they may say they are ok, but you're not convinced. In this case, continue to keep an eye on them – this is an amber light. If they do get worse, they may feel that they can talk to you then.

Whether or not they are okay, it is helpful to ask. It can be reassuring to know someone is looking out for you – the sense of isolation is often harsh when unwell.

If you have a serious concern that they may harm themselves – speak to someone else about it.

EXPLORE: Remember you are not the expert

Having listened, what should you do with the information? You need to do surprisingly little – remember, unless you have training and experience as a mental health practitioner, you are not the expert. This part of the NILE process is simply exploring with the other person what they can do, and signposting where to go next for appropriate help.

It's tempting to try and help, to offer solutions, and this impulse can come from a good place; but unless you have training and experience, steer away from this. Unsubstantiated advice, sharing one's own ideas, or conclusions from loosely related experience is unlikely to be useful. At best it is neutral and at worst it can unintentionally invalidate what the other person is saying, making it harder for them to get the help they actually need.

It can help to acknowledge that you don't know the answer!

Think about it in terms of a physical health issue – if someone has a broken leg you might ask how it happened, talk about it, acknowledge it, even offer to sign the plaster! If someone has a nasty cough, you might ask if they are taking anything for it or if they have been to the doctor. Approaching mental ill health in the same matter-of-fact way can help open up the conversation.

Again, some suggested questions and phrases may help. You could ask, "Have you seen your GP?" or "Who can you talk to?" or "Have you spoken to anyone?"

You can go on to ask, "What are you going to do?" so that a plan is in place. To let them know you'll be keeping an eye out for them, you might say, "If it's OK, I'll check in with you on..." and say when that is. If you offer to check in, make sure you do!

As mentioned, this stage is about exploring what the person can do themselves and you may have noticed that these are steps that they identify themselves. As a non-expert, any "advice" should be limited to signposting – helpful signposts might be HR, Mental Health First Aiders, their GP, friends and family, or organizations such as LawCare.

If someone says they are suicidal, stay with them and tell them that you are going to get help from HR. Assure them that this will be on a confidential basis.

Conclusion

The NILE model is an entry-point into normalizing conversations about mental health. While we are all learning to do this, these conversations will by their nature be awkward. It's only by having them – and even by having conversations about having the conversation – that we will get any better at them.

I suggest a first step of discussing this chapter with a friend or colleague – start by having a conversation about having the conversation.

Note to the reader

If you're reading this and thinking, "Yes, but *I* am unwell," my answer is, "If you are ill, you can be well again. There is no shame in your illness. Please speak with someone and ask for help."

For me it was essential to get help and useful to get a diagnosis. The standard classification and diagnostic guide for mental disorders is known as DSM5 and is often criticized for taking a top-down approach by attempting to fit patients into fairly rigid criteria, rather than starting with their symptoms.

However, when I became aware of the diagnostic criteria for depression – YES, they were gloomy: key symptoms such as losing interest in what you enjoy, being fatigued... and a minor symptom that included wanting to be dead! BUT – it was reassuring to know it was from a textbook. I realized that if I was just ill, then I could be well again and it normalized my illness. That was a turning point for me, realizing that I didn't need to feel shame for being ill – I didn't need to be silent.

Asking for help

At the time of my return to work, I was not completely well. I had discussed this with my psychiatrist – I was at the point where I was well enough to be at work, but not yet fully recovered.

As a freelancer, I did not disclose this to my client – because of the fear of the judgements that might be made about my ability to fulfil my role and be given further freelance work, as well as about me as a flawed and inferior human being. In that particular role, I wrote and presented online continuing professional development programs *and my role included interviewing experts in the field about developments in the law. Unfortunately, my memory had been affected and I was terrified of forgetting my interview questions, even though I kept these as short and simple as I could.*

I waited until the fear was unbearable and outweighed the risk of not being given further freelance programs. *Finally, I confided in my line manager, and I was lucky that she was* non-judgmental *and open. We worked out a system in case I did forget a question: I would give a subtle signal to the producer in the viewing gallery, who had my list of questions and they would feed the next question to me though my earpiece. As it turned out, I didn't need the safety net.*

I was lucky that the person I spoke to did not make assumptions about my capacity or capability and that we were able to work on the solution collaboratively.

Workplaces are evolving and many of them are able to offer help. If discussing it in your workplace feels too risky for you, then look outside the workplace; but please speak to *someone* because support will be available for you. Asking for help takes courage, but it is worth it in releasing the pressure and this is not something you need to do on your own.

References

1. https://assets.publishing.service.gov.uk/government/uploads/system/uploads/attachment_data/file/658145/thriving-at-work-stevenson-farmer-review.pdf
2. www.beyondblue.org.au/
3. https://mhfaengland.org/
4. www.livingworks.net/safetalk
5. https://v-sense.scss.tcd.ie/news/bridging-the-blue-open-quarter-2019-folkestone-uk/
6. www.who.int/mental_health/en/
7. www.researchgate.net/publication/303540780_Increase_Strength_and_Mood_with_Posture
8. https://med.stanford.edu/news/all-news/2017/03/study-discovers-how-slow-breathing-induces-tranquility.html
9. www.time-to-change.org.uk/asktwice

Chapter 6:
Creating psychological safety

By Matt Dean, byrne·dean

I write this chapter very much from a hands-on perspective. In my day job I regularly interview leaders, facilitate discussions about workplace behavior, and conduct what clients insist on calling remedial coaching sessions (with people who've got things wrong in terms of harassment and behavior). I have clear ideas about what works. I talk to people about their accountability and about changing the bit of the firm they influence. It doesn't matter who they are, everyone has influence.

I spent 14 years working in two major London law firms. I left in 2003 to set up byrne·dean and have since then spent almost every day thinking, talking, and writing about creating kinder, fairer, more productive workplaces – often in law firms. I'm indebted to Richard Martin (who wrote the introduction to this book) for much of how I now think about and understand mental health as it relates to workplaces, particularly in law firms. Which isn't to say that I don't have my own lived experience of mental ill health, both my own and in my immediate family. Richard joined byrne·dean in 2013. Shortly after that we agreed that a major goal for us could be effecting change in law firms. Neither of us felt that they had quite got it right yet.

Storytelling plays a massively important part in all successful culture change. Early on, Richard and I swapped our stories of what happened to us when we first came out as junior lawyers who were struggling to cope in our respective law firms. Both of us chose to come out at a time (20 plus years ago) when that sort of thing wasn't really done.

Richard was still an articled clerk (as we used to be known) and certainly proficient because too much was expected of him. The pressure of work meant that Richard wasn't sleeping and was feeling overwhelmed. He decided that he had to say something to the senior associate he was working most closely with. He arrived at work bright and early. Unfortunately the person he'd chosen to talk to had a reputation for arriving late. So Richard waited, ineffectually pushing things round his desk while keeping an eye out. Finally, Richard sat down with him and blurted out that he wasn't sleeping, that he had far too much on, that he didn't know what to do.

Richard described the laidback associate's initial reaction as being… calm. He nodded and smiled, empathetically. He held his hands out in a gesture of containment. He gave Richard a simple instruction: *"Tell me: what's the most pressing thing that you have got to do today?"* Richard knew instinctively and answered immediately. The partner said, *"Ok, go and do that. Do it well and then come back and see me."* Richard described a weight lifting as the clarity enveloped him. He went off and did the thing. He was no longer overwhelmed.

When we traded stories, so many years later, Richard wasn't even sure if he had returned for more instructions later that morning. He knew what he had to do.

My story is slightly different. I was probably five years qualified, maybe six. I was in my second law firm and hadn't yet developed good, trusting relationships with those around me. Those relationships did come later, but they hadn't formed yet. Nor did I feel very comfortable with most of the work I was doing. For someone of my qualification I was inexperienced in many of the things regarded as standard in my new firm. I knew employment tribunal litigation and little else. I was also struggling to supervise my (challenging) trainee with any level of authority.

Most pressingly, I was running something high profile for a partner who was seldom in the office. I had to produce a note of a recent consultation with a silk and I frankly hadn't understood the discussion. I didn't know who to talk to about it. I am now and already was then a poor sleeper. Normally though, after one poor night I will sleep the second night. On this occasion it was on the third night of not sleeping that things started to unravel for me.

In the middle of that third night I formed the view that I had to tell someone. I chose the most approachable partner. It took courage. Or maybe it didn't. Maybe I'd decided during that third sleepless night that I couldn't do the job. I remember clearly walking into the room, the sun streaming through the window. I remember that the partner looked busy, distracted. It never occurred to me that they may not be sleeping either. I pressed on. I sat down. I apologized and said that I wasn't coping.

The response came pretty quickly: *"Really Matt. [Slight pause]… I hadn't noticed."* The tone was sarcastic and the impact immediate. I got up to walk out – I knew there was no point. I felt sick. I was close to tears. The partner stopped me, but our conversation was short and went nowhere; I felt like I had made a mistake and probably damaged my career. I have no clarity about what happened next – I probably muddled through. The incident stuck though.

Looking back at that moment from a distance of 20 plus years, I want to say first that I'm now absolutely clear that poor leader behavior is almost always not intentional. The leader probably doesn't feel safe themselves – they may not be able to raise their concerns with the people around them. I can now see that partner was working under immense pressure – certainly it was far greater than the pressure I was under. They were probably struggling to see a way out of the situation they were in.

But the story is the story, the impact was the impact.

If I was only able to give people one message about creating psychological safety, it would be that they need to focus on the impact they are having on the people around them, on the conversations that they have (or don't have). You can always find a way of justifying or explaining your behavior. Perhaps you can barely cope with what is being thrown at you, or the person coming to you is just not up to it, or you think about how you were treated when you were at their stage, etc. Those justifications are natural and they foster psychologically unsafe environments.

When you strip culture down, it's basically the conversations that people have in a workplace every day. Culture is about how willing people are to have the conversations, the tone of those conversations, and the impact they have on the people who have them. Changing the culture is actually about changing those conversations, getting people to prioritize the impact they are having.

What actually is psychological safety?

Psychological safety feels like an idea that's emerged from the shadows in recent years. Possibly not quite as obviously as the idea of mental health – which has been catapulted from the shadows of stigma to the center of public (and private) discourse. Both are ideas whose time has come. What interests me is how the ideas have developed separately, despite being possibly inextricably linked.

In my book, *The Soft Stuff: reclaiming kindness for the world of work,* I write in some detail about Google's gargantuan research project – Aristotle. In 2012 the tech giant embarked on a quest to find out "*What makes a team effective at Google?*" After four years of enormous investment, in 2016 the Aristotle team published the idea that effectiveness was more about *how* a team works together than the mix of individuals who make up the team.

Of the five key team dynamics their researchers identified, *psychological safety* was in their view by far the most important.

In 1999, Amy Edmondson at Harvard Business School first identified the concept as "*A sense of confidence that the team will not embarrass, reject or punish someone for speaking up*". Interpersonal trust and mutual respect characterized this climate of safety in which people could be themselves.

Both my and Richard's stories come from around the turn of the century – the sort of time Edmondson first wrote about psychological safety. It was a time when mental health wasn't talked about, certainly not in law firms. We just got on with our sometimes hugely challenging work and workloads. Some of us floated and many sank.

I'm not sure whether Richard was aware that he was in a psychologically safe environment, but apparently he was. He spoke up and he wasn't embarrassed, rejected, or punished for doing so. He had been himself and he was shown respect. My experience was different – for about a year it hadn't felt to me that I was in a particularly safe environment. In that moment in the partner's office that fact was confirmed to me.

Like many others I'm sure, I hadn't heard the term psychological safety before 2016. I had talked for years, probably almost every day, about either the importance of trust and respect (and particularly about what respect actually looks like). I also regularly talked about people being more productive when they are able to be themselves at work, about happy people working harder. It was just the label of psychological safety that was missing.

Today, I regularly ask leaders (often hugely successful people) to go back to a moment in their career when they weren't developing, when they might even have been going backwards. What's striking for me is that, prompted by a story like mine, virtually all successful leaders will talk about a moment or time (in fact, probably more than one) in their own career when things were misfiring. Sometimes quite badly. Often they talk about the lack of a relationship with their boss(es).

Building psychological safety – conversation by conversation

Much has happened in law firms since my experience, but junior lawyers still don't feel psychologically safe at work – the surveys tell us that. Edmondson saw psychological safety as being underpinned by interpersonal trust and mutual respect. I don't think that I'd be speaking out of turn if I said that in many of the professional services firms I've worked recently, the relationship between partners and associates isn't often one that you would immediately describe as being one of trust and mutual respect.

If we also accept the premise that culture is built conversation by conversation, the simple, pertinent question becomes, *"What conversations build a psychologically safe culture?"*

Thinking back to my own experience, the first answer I would give is simple. I wasn't having any authentic, human conversations with the people in authority. Any such contact would have had enormous impact on how I felt. I was feeling isolated, alone, and excluded – there was an in group and I wasn't in it. I was not feeling respected – personally or professionally – or trusted (which I think is a higher bar).

If one of those people would have built a bridge by saying to me, *"If you're ever worried or out of your depth, come and see me. Call me if I'm not here. That's really important to me,"* I would have felt far safer. Provided I believed them. This is about authenticity; again, it's a relatively new concept. I'm not sure how much it really adds to be human.

In a catch up over coffee with someone I work with recently she said of our (admittedly very irregular) conversations, *"I get the real you"*. That really resonated with me. I've never intellectualized how I am, and how I behave, when I sit down with people. However, I think and talk about this sort of thing every day. Also instinctively, possibly because of my experiences, being myself, sharing my innermost thoughts, feels like the right thing to do.

Actually, there's a bit more to it than being yourself. My colleague elaborated, *"It doesn't feel like you've got an agenda, a checklist, it feels like you're listening to me. If I raise something big, I think you'll deal with it."* Conversational turn taking, each person feeling that they get a chance to raise their perspective, is often talked about as being part of psychological safety, as is social sensitivity. The turn taking doesn't just happen – you have to want to hear what the other person is going to say, and often you have to structure the conversation, particularly in a group setting.

When I suggest to most leaders I work with (particularly the law firm partners) that they have to want to hear from their associates, they leak fear into our conversation. They will say something that sounds like, *"But what if they tell me something I don't want to hear"* or *"I can't solve all their problems"*. They are afraid of getting too close to someone, of that person sharing their innermost fears and expecting resolution. I try to reassure them that the other person isn't expecting you to solve their problems, they want you to make them feel listened to and at some level valued in their work. That will make a huge difference to them. They could also be looking for something that will help them deal with the problem they currently have – like the advice Richard got to prioritize.

Particularly in a law firm, shortly after sharing the fear that they'll hear something they can't handle, most leaders will bring up the idea of the other person's capability. They will ask, "*What if they are just not up to it!?*" In fact, that may even come up first. I've already said that the poor performance label is often used by leaders to justify what could be termed sub-optimal leadership behavior on their part.

In settings with expectations of high performance, we label people quickly. I characterize the default leadership behavior frequently described to me as "*see poor performance, think poor performer*". The idea is closely aligned to performance attribution error – the way that we attribute poor performance in others to intrinsic weaknesses they may have while we would attribute similar failings in ourselves to extrinsic factors.

This labelling is neither logical nor rational (which ironically are both things that lawyers would say they prize). First, without exception, all of the law firm executive committees I've worked with have worried about the high cost of their retention levels. Yet the partners of those firms all label compulsively, which inevitably will increase rates of turnover. Perhaps more importantly, it's an absolute truth that to have got into the sort of firm we're talking about, the poor performer must have shown remarkable levels of intellectual achievement, academic performance, and personal resilience.

These are exceptional people who have been chosen from hundreds of applicants because they have shown real potential. Yet at the first sign of weakness, we label them as poor performers or not cut out for this. In my mind, any successful challenge to this negative pigeon-holing of talent requires each leader to understand that no one's level of performance is set in stone. In recent years this single thought has underpinned a whole philosophy – that of growth mindset.

No one is simply a *poor performer.* However, chances are they'll become one if you label and treat them as one. The truth is that the primary driver of workplace behavior and performance is how the person currently feels in their work environment.

An easy way to get leaders to grasp this central idea (that how someone feels drives how they perform) is the storytelling exercise I mentioned earlier. Get leaders to think about that time in their own career when they weren't developing – tell them stories and get them telling stories. If we're one-to-one they can tell me their stories; if we're in a group they can tell someone they buddy with. Chances are, when they were struggling, they were also not performing anywhere near their best. I certainly wasn't.

Crucially, if you want them to change their behavior, make sure to get them to focus on and to name the emotions they were experiencing at that time. Stories unlock emotions and it's those emotions that will drive any future change in actions. If you want someone to change the conversations they have in the workplace, start with getting them to focus on how they felt when things weren't going well for them (or when they were going incredibly well – which is another exercise).

Do lawyers have the social sensitivity skills to do this?

If I may, another story. In 2015 I was running a session with about 12 partners in an international law firm. About 20 minutes into it one of them said (and I think this is pretty much word for word):

> *"You do know what we do here, don't you: we're lawyers, we do law. It's just that you've been talking for 20 minutes about emotions and I can't see where we're going with this. You are either good at law or you're not."*

I sensed that one or two of his colleagues agreed with him (and didn't want to be in the room). I also sensed that some of the others there – the ones who started to drive the debate from that point – were embarrassed that one of them could have expressed the view. Remember, in a psychologically safe environment, everyone must be able to be themselves, to raise their questions. That's also a very important part of successful culture change.

Some of the hundreds of lawyers I've worked with and known well are, I am pretty sure, high functioning autistic or somewhere on a spectrum of that type. It's an idea that came to me from psychologists I've worked with. But, the vast majority of them are human beings who in their personal and family lives are completely capable of showing empathy, asking great questions, listening and helping someone else to see what they need to do.

Imagine, for example, one of their friends telling them over a coffee that they were having difficulty finding elder care for their ageing and recently bereaved parent. They would express concern, ask questions that would focus the other's mind, listen and help solve. These are the sort of skills that lawyers have. They're also the skills you need when someone comes to you at work saying they can't cope.

The problem is that leaders often don't think of using these skills at work, because they haven't recognized how important their associates' or peers' emotional wellbeing is to the performance of the firm. It's our job to get them to see that and to be comfortable using those skills. The challenge is to prioritize the soft stuff.

Some rules might help?

Project Aristotle had other findings too. The one that will almost certainly support psychological safety the most obviously is *structure and clarity* – are goals, roles, and execution plans clear? It's critically important that we devote time and attention to this. Also to the way that we provide feedback.

At byrne·dean we have five rules for effective feedback. I just want to go over two of them here. The first is very simple: if sitting down with someone is not a genuine attempt to improve them or help them develop, don't bother! You have to *want* to be creating that positive change. This is number one for good reason. Trust underpins psychological safety and much else. It's the single most important element of a positive workplace relationship.

Focus for a moment on the people, the leaders, that you've trusted most in workplaces. Who were they? I often ask this question of people. There's a piece about trusted leaders delivering what they promise. But normally there's something more important – the most trusted leaders are the people who want to develop you, to make you better. It doesn't matter what their motivation is for this. The two people I trusted most in a law firm setting both told me explicitly that me developing into the person they were planning would help them greatly. What's not to like? It's a win-win, we're in this together.

I typically suggest to leaders that in feedback meetings and the like they should be more explicit about what their role is: *"Remember the reason we're sitting here/what I am trying to do is to make you into the best* [IP litigator or whatever] *you can be"*. If you actually are trying to do that, please say it. Always remember though, rule #1 is don't bother unless it is a genuine attempt.

Another one of the rules, and one that chimes with psychological safety, is ask, don't tell. You want the person in front of you to create some new way of looking at something – technically a schema or neural pathway. The easiest way to do that is not through a well-crafted and possibly rehearsed speech, the first stanza of which the other person will inevitably disagree with! We've all been there, being lectured by someone who hasn't done our job for years and who's telling us where we've gone wrong.

The easiest way to create a new neural pathway is to use carefully crafted, open questions that will unlock debate. I always suggest that leaders decide on the development areas they want to raise in a conversation and then think of a good open question to start the debate in each development area. Then they must listen (to understand) to what the other person says – actually listen and probe. You may find out what's on their mind. They may change their mind. They'll certainly feel valued.

There's a much bigger problem – time!

Time is the enemy of all people management. We'd all love to have the time to do the soft stuff, but we have to do our day jobs instead. It's what pays the bills. The truth is that the bills get paid when we have engaged associates delivering remarkable results. Once leaders understand that the key to this is psychological safety, they may prioritize their relationships with the people they rely on. Again, that's an important part of the job.

Some further rules?

Are there any rules about interventions to help leaders change the conversations they have? Certainly. Having been involved in hundreds of interventions, I've tried to come up with a few simple rules.

1. **Ideally we will have enunciated our purpose as a firm (or possibly a department or team)** – everyone will be clear why we exist and our direction of travel. If they see psychological safety as being obviously consistent with that direction, the job of changing the conversations they have becomes far easier.
2. **There'll be obvious and genuine support from senior leadership** – ideally this will take the form of your chosen senior leaders telling their own personal stories as part of the intervention. The most successful change programs are the ones in which important and influential people have invested personal capital. That basically means that if the initiative bombs, the leader will look less good. This obviously makes it more difficult to find leaders to make the investment. But look, for example, at how success in the mental health arena in recent years has been underpinned by so many leaders being brave and being the change they want to see.

   There's been no shortage of leaders taking risks and talking about their commitment to mental health. Take a leaf from something like "*This is me*" and get an authentic endorsement of psychological safety. Find leaders willing to talk about conversations that people had with them (or that they have had with others) and how they felt as people after those conversations (both the good and the bad).
3. **Individual leaders will buy in if they understand a) how they are going to benefit and b) what's required of them** – each leader's

understanding of what's required of them should be in granular detail, at what you might call the conversational level: *"When you want to have a conversation about performance, you could…"* or *"When someone says to you that they are not coping, you could…"*.

Less successful engagements in my experience tend to leave things at a more theoretical/general level; these interventions can amount to little more than a checklist telling people what they can/should do – the sort of conversations that they should be having. Leaders can choose to engage or not in what is often called a cascade. If leaders are going to have the required level of understanding and a mindset to deliver change, they need more than to be told what to do.

A successful engagement with leaders will resonate at an emotional level; it will encourage and inspire participants and help them work out how to translate the messages they're receiving into day-to-day actions. The power of drama-based learning, allowing them to practice and to watch their colleagues practicing with real people, cannot be overstated.

4. **Use storytelling** – think of a time in your life when you did or didn't have the sort of conversation that creates psychological safety. That's what will resonate with people at the emotional level and help them to shape their own goals and benchmarks. Successful culture change encourages this exchange – you create change by creating and telling stories.

5. **Work with everyone** – yes, work with the leaders, but remember that we all have influence. As part of the change, get the entire population in a room or rooms. Get them talking to each other about what we are trying to achieve. Tell them stories and get them thinking about the stories they can tell. Give them confidence to talk if they are not feeling safe; show them that there is a path to follow; talk to them about the sort of conversations they could have in that moment.

A very important part of the message to anyone feeling unsafe is that the person who is making them feel unsafe almost certainly is not doing so intentionally. They are just not focusing on the impact that they are having. It is this single idea – of getting people to focus on the impact that they are having – that probably lies at the center of a successful engagement.

Chapter 7:
Junior lawyers and mental ill health

By Kayleigh Leonie, trustee, LawCare

This chapter summarizes and analyses the research undertaken by the Junior Lawyers Division of The Law Society of England and Wales into the negative stress and mental ill health experienced by junior lawyers in the profession. It looks at the causes and effects of the stress junior lawyers are experiencing and considers the positive measures put in place by individuals and employers to alleviate that stress, many of which are included in the recommendations set out in The Law Society's best practice guidance for employers on supporting wellbeing in the workplace. It also draws upon the insights obtained through a series of roundtables held with law firms in the City of London from 2018 to explore best practice.

Starting your career in law

When starting a legal career, whether as a paralegal, legal apprentice, or trainee solicitor, it is likely to be an individual's first time working in a professional environment. As well as adjusting to working in the legal profession, paralegals, legal apprentices, and trainee solicitors are under an increased amount of pressure as they try to prove themselves to their employers, either to be awarded a much sought after training position, or to be offered a newly-qualified position at the end of it. As a result of these challenges, many junior lawyers feel unable to raise issues with their employers when they are struggling to cope with the pressures of their role. It can be difficult to juggle your workload, particularly in circumstances where, as a junior, you are accepting work from a number of colleagues, more senior than you, in the department.

The transition from trainee to becoming a newly qualified solicitor can also be a tricky one, as you try to establish yourself in the department you have qualified into. This can come with its own complications and additional pressure as many junior lawyers have a tendency to worry and over-prepare when they are released from the protective shield of being a trainee. Perfectionism and imposter syndrome are known to be problematic in the profession.

Junior lawyer research

In 2017, the Junior Lawyers Division (JLD) of The Law Society of England and Wales developed a survey for junior lawyers to gather data on the levels of negative stress[1] and mental ill health[2] experienced by junior lawyers. For the purposes of the survey, "junior lawyers" includes paralegals who have obtained or are studying for their legal practice course, trainee solicitors, and solicitors with up to five years post-qualification experience.

The survey ran from 2017 to 2019[3] and the number of respondents increased year on year from 214 responses in 2017, 959 in 2018 and 1,803 in the most recent 2019 survey. The results of the surveys have received significant coverage across the legal press in England and Wales and are regularly cited in articles on the topics of stress and mental health.

Interestingly, in each year that the survey ran, over 70 percent of the junior lawyers responding were female. This is not only disproportionate to the number of male and female solicitors on the roll during this time (48.7 percent male, 51.3 percent female)[4] but also to the number of male and female solicitors holding practicing certificates, zero to nine years since admission (40 percent male, 60 percent female).[5]

Negative stress experienced by junior lawyers

The results of the surveys over the last three years has been consistent, with over 90 percent of junior lawyers experiencing negative stress at work with over a quarter feeling severely or extremely stressed. For the purpose of the survey, stress was defined as being under too much emotional or mental pressure.

To focus on the results of the most recent 2019 survey, over 90 percent of respondents worked in private practice with just over 30 percent working with vulnerable clients[6] and over a quarter working in the City of London. A higher proportion of junior lawyers working with vulnerable clients reported "regularly" feeling unable to cope (22.9 percent) compared to those not working for this client group (17.3 percent). Qualified solicitors were the group most likely to report experiencing severe or extreme levels of work-related stress (27 percent) compared to 20 percent of trainees and 22 percent of paralegals. It appears from the results that the additional responsibility of practicing as a solicitor, rather than being supervised as a trainee or paralegal, adds to the negative stress experienced. The sample size of those working as paralegals and trainees was, however, much smaller than those working as qualified solicitors.

Interestingly, a higher proportion of solicitors working in small firms reported regularly feeling unable to cope (28.8 percent) compared to those working in the larger (26+ partner firms) (16.7 percent). Larger firms are likely to have more resources in place for their employees, which help them to feel more supported in the workplace – for example, whole departments of support functions such as dedicated human resources teams and IT/document production teams and access to an employee assistance program or providing private medical insurance that gives employees access to therapy sessions.

The most frequently cited causes of work-related stress were high workload, client demands and expectations, lack of support, and ineffective management. Other factors included a number of people-related issues (such as attitudes and behaviors of colleagues and supervisors, a lack of supervision and a lack of feedback) and work-related issues (such as a poor office culture, long hours and a lack of training). Each of these factors is within an employer's control to change providing it is able to understand the root cause of the issues and put measures in place to combat them and relieve the stress they are putting on employees.

When asking respondents about the effects of work-related stress, in the open-text responses to the 2018 survey a number of respondents mentioned self-harm and experiencing suicidal thoughts. The 2019 survey therefore included self-harm as part of the response on stress having a negative impact on mental health and separately a response on experiencing suicidal thoughts. Alarmingly, one in 15 junior lawyers reported experienced suicidal thoughts as a result of stress at work in the month before completing the survey.

As a result of the levels of stress experienced by junior lawyers, over 65 percent reported experiencing disrupted sleep, nearly 60 percent reported it having a negative effect on their mental health (anxiety, emotional upset, fatigue, negative and depressed thoughts, self-harm), and almost 35 percent had experienced problems with family life or relationships as a result.

It is notable that in the 2017 survey almost 74 percent of respondents said that their employer should be doing more to provide help, guidance, and support in relation to stress at work and this has increased to over 83 percent in 2018 and over 71 percent in 2019. There is still therefore a considerable amount junior lawyers expect their employers to be doing to help them feel more supported at work.

As lawyers, most of us would say that we work well under pressure and that we need some pressure in order to perform at our best. Unfortunately, when that pressure turns into negative stress it adversely affects our performance and efficiency. Experiencing prolonged periods of stress can have a negative impact on mental and physical health.

Mental ill health experienced by junior lawyers

The number of junior lawyers experiencing mental ill health (whether formally diagnosed or not) in the month before completing the survey increased considerably to 48 percent in the 2019 survey (from the 26 percent reported in the 2017 survey and 38.5 percent reported in the 2018 survey). The sharp increase in numbers could be down to a number of things, including people being better informed about mental ill health and so being able to recognize it in themselves. It may also be due to the effect of the industry trying to reduce the stigma surrounding mental health and, perhaps to a certain extent, those responding to a survey titled "resilience and wellbeing survey" being more likely to experience mental ill health. It is clear that the increase at this rate is alarming and, as reported in a number of articles in the press, the legal profession could be on the verge of a mental health crisis.[7]

Focusing on the results of the most recent 2019 survey, over half (53 percent) of those working with vulnerable clients reported experiencing mental ill health compared to 46 percent of those not working with this client group. It appears therefore that there may not be sufficient training in place for junior lawyers working with vulnerable clients to ensure that they are given the skills they need to support themselves when supporting this client group.

Nearly three-quarters (74 percent) of those experiencing mental ill health reported disrupted sleep. In a profession known for its long working hours, it is concerning that when junior lawyers are trying to sleep, it is disrupted. Almost 60 percent of junior lawyers reported their mental ill health having a negative impact on their physical health (feeling physically sick, chest pains). A number of respondents also mentioned experiencing panic attacks, tension headaches, repetitive anxious thoughts and recurrent nightmares. Such negative experiences led many junior lawyers to resign and seek medical help whilst others reported taking prescribed medication for depression/anxiety.

As a result of experiencing mental ill health, over a quarter of respondents (28.4 percent) admitted making a mistake that would not otherwise have happened and 38.6 percent reported nearly making a mistake that would not have otherwise happened. The first press coverage received by the survey back in 2017 focused on the risk for law firms having overworked lawyers more likely to make mistakes.[8]

Interestingly, only one in five junior lawyer respondents had told their employer about experiencing mental ill health with a higher proportion of female junior lawyers (21 percent) compared to male junior lawyers (14 percent) reporting their employer was aware. It is noteworthy that even though lots more is being done year on year to try to alleviate the negative stigma of mental health, most junior lawyers do not feel comfortable or do not want to tell their employer about what they are dealing with. If junior lawyers do not feel able to report experiencing mental ill health to their employers, they are not only missing out on being able to obtain additional support (if their employer is prepared to put measures in place), but they are also at risk of falling short of expectations and being penalized as a result.

Over 78 percent of junior lawyers (and 87 percent of those experiencing mental ill health) said that their employer could do more to provide help, support, and guidance in relation to mental health in the workplace (a significant increase from 50 percent in 2017). It is good to know that around three-fifths (62 percent) of junior lawyers were aware of organizations that were there to help if they wanted to discuss stress at work or any other mental health concerns.

Supporting yourself as a junior lawyer

In order to manage or reduce the stress experienced at work, the most common mechanism cited by junior lawyers was exercising – although many complained of being too exhausted to do so. Others used meditation techniques and breathing exercises including mindfulness to help them refocus and prioritize their wellbeing. There were lots of comments on incorporating techniques to manage workload, for example, breaking tasks down, creating to-do lists, pushing back on deadlines, and being realistic on what could be achieved. Many advised that they had spoken to family, friends, or their partner to express feelings, share problems, or ask for support. It was good to see some junior lawyers commenting that they had spoken to a manager, partner, or supervisor to ask for help.

The 2019 survey asked junior lawyers what their employer was currently doing to support their levels of stress and mental health at work and what more they thought their employer could be doing. Many junior lawyers reported that the issue was simply being ignored, even in circumstances where they were signed off work as a result of mental ill health. Many commented on the stigma around mental health, which is still prevalent in the legal profession, and that support from senior members of staff was not consistent.

Best practice in the workplace

In order to address the concerning results of the surveys in respect of the lack of action taken by employers in the legal profession, the JLD decided to prepare best practice guidance for employers to support good wellbeing in the workplace. The guidance was initially released by the JLD in February 2018 on Time to Talk Day[9] and was subsequently revised and re-launched by The Law Society on World Mental Health Day in October 2019.[10]

The best practice guidance is designed to give employers ideas on how to build a successful wellbeing strategy for their organization. The guidance focuses on three core pillars – support, education and training, and culture, to enable organizational change. In order for an organization to successfully make changes, it needs to understand how its employees would define its culture, whether this matches the culture the organization is trying to achieve, and what changes or new initiatives its employees want to see introduced to support their wellbeing.

In very brief summary, the recommendations surrounding the three core pillars include the following (a number of these recommendations are also considered in more detail later on).

Support

Implementing a work council/employee engagement group, introducing a champions/guardians program, training mental health first aiders, obtaining an employee assistance program/counselling service, undertaking stress risk assessments, following the Health and Safety Executive's guidance, appointing a wellbeing committee, introducing a mentoring program, starting health promotion initiatives, encouraging employee-led groups, utilizing occupational health, reviewing sickness absence policies, creating a handover policy, informing employees of external charities/advice lines, reviewing internal system/processes, introducing de-briefs after transactions/matters are finalized, and showcasing key dates for flagship events.

Education and training

Training line managers, discussing individual training needs with employees, encouraging regular and constructive feedback, ensuring sufficient supervision, encapsulating wellbeing within performance reviews, ensuring employees working in human resources have received appropriate training, arranging seminars, running workshops, inviting guest speakers, and incorporating a wellbeing strategy into policies and procedures that are flagged to employees as part of their induction.

Culture

Sharing personal stories, appointing champions/mentors, amending or preparing an organization commitment statement, encouraging a leadership-led approach, fostering a positive culture, introducing a culture code, ensuring a joined-up approach across the organization, encouraging employees to take annual leave/time away from the office, supporting self-care, looking at employees' working hours and breaks, considering changes to support digital wellbeing, ensuring effective communication, addressing presenteeism/leaveism, challenging deadlines, considering billable hours targets, introducing agile working, monitoring success, introducing peer support, fostering a culture of owning up to mistakes, making processes more efficient, and ensuring reward links to fostering a positive culture.

Having sought feedback from junior lawyers working across the profession, the revised guidance includes a page of behaviors and changes to look out for in employees, which may flag to you that they are not coping and that they may need your support. It includes two cartoons that play out good and bad ways to deal with having a conversation on wellbeing with a colleague in a more considerate and effective way and the importance of active listening when having a conversation with a colleague. It can be difficult to strike up a conversation with someone in the office and respect professional boundaries so it is important to remember that we are all human. Being compassionate to others in the workplace is essential to build successful working relations so we should not be afraid to check in on our colleagues when we are concerned about them.

The guidance also breaks down the recommendations to those applicable for employers of all sizes and for those most likely to be applicable for medium- and large-sized organizations, and includes case studies from employers across the country that showcase the work they have been doing to support the wellbeing of their employees in the workplace.

Mentally healthy workplaces

As part of encouraging employers to embrace wellbeing at work and implement the recommendations in the best practice guidance, a roundtable series was set up for law firms in the City of London. The roundtables began in March 2018 with the aim of giving law firms an opportunity to learn about different wellbeing topics and to create a network of firms across the city to share best practice, knowledge, and the challenges being faced when implementing wellbeing initiatives. These roundtables have become a forum in which representatives from across the legal profession can share their experiences with each other to drive forward healthy workplace culture across the profession.

There are a number of recommendations in the best practice guidance, which have been discussed as part of the roundtables over the last two years, which are considered in greater detail below.

Storytelling

Encouraging employees at all levels, in particular senior employees, across an organization to speak up and share their own personal stories is very empowering, not only for those listening but for the person having the courage to share their experiences of dealing with mental ill health. It is a great way to help break down any stigmas associated with mental health and build trust across an organization. It also encourages employees to be more open about their own mental health and wellbeing. Some law firms have launched internal blogs to share employees' posts and others have invited employees to speak at internal events to share their stories. Many employees who have not themselves been directly affected by mental ill health have chosen to share the experiences of somebody close to them and how it has impacted their own wellbeing. Having senior employees opening up about mental ill health and setting a clear example for more junior employees is key for an organization to ensure that there is a genuine commitment to supporting good wellbeing in the workplace.

Wellbeing policy

Creating an internal wellbeing policy is a great way for an organization to evaluate its culture and see what its employees understand its core values to be. It ensures a joined-up approach across the organization and it enables the organization to be clear on its strategy and future developments. A wellbeing policy should not only embed the organization's core values, it should also make recommendations on how all aspects of work should be approached with wellbeing at the heart. By getting employees involved in developing the policy at the outset, this will encourage engagement and ensure there are advocates across the organization to champion the policy.

In terms of what a wellbeing policy can include, it should set out ways in which the organization is supporting employees' wellbeing, what employees should do to raise wellbeing concerns for themselves and others, and how an employee can call out unhelpful practices that do not adhere to the wellbeing policy and the organization's values. It should explain how employees are expected to work with each other in accordance with the organization's values. It can also act as a central point to signpost employees to all of the other wellbeing resources available. As with all policies, it is very important that all employees know about their existence (they should therefore form part of the induction process).

It is not as simple as creating a wellbeing policy; organizations need to practice what they preach by ensuring that it is being adhered to by employees at all levels of the organization. In addition, organizations should ensure that all other internal policies and procedures, for example sickness absence procedures, are implemented on a case-by-case basis, taking into account each employee's personal circumstances. All policies and procedures should be reviewed and updated where necessary. By way of example, we have seen a shift in law firms revising their internal alcohol procedures to move away from them being solely disciplinary in nature and instead incorporating guidance on how to create a healthy drinking culture in the workplace with the focus of events not being around consuming alcohol.

Rest

Having the ability to switch off from work is key to ensuring employees are able to practice self-care to ensure they can relax and recuperate. The legal profession is renowned for its long working hours culture with strict client deadlines and demands, meaning it is one of the most difficult things for an organization to manage. It is imperative that employers, managers, and human resources understand the importance of downtime and switching off from work to maintain good mental and physical health.

In order for employees to perform at their best, it is important that they are encouraged to take regular breaks during the working day and leave their desks to avoid being distracted by work.

Employees need to maintain boundaries between their personal and working lives to ensure that they have proper down-time away from work to rest and maximize their personal relationships and interests which are vital to their wellbeing (and sustainable long-term performance). Organizations should therefore ensure that their employees are able (and encouraged) to switch off from work when on annual leave. Human resources and/or managers should play an important role in checking that their employees are using their annual leave entitlement. Preparing to take holiday can be stressful in itself so employers should have guidelines in place for arranging handovers when employees do take leave, which can form part of the organization's wellbeing policy,

If an organization is committed to creating a healthy and resilient workplace, it should be prepared to challenge presenteeism (where people insist on working when they are physically or mentally unwell) and leaveism (where people continue to work whilst on holiday) to ensure employees do not feel obliged to work in circumstances where they are unwell or on holiday.

In more general terms, managers should also encourage employees to leave the office when they have finished their work and should not tolerate a culture whereby junior employees feel that they are unable to leave the office before their supervisors for fear of negative repercussions.

Reward

Some law firms are now incorporating wellbeing into employees' performance reviews, which is a positive step to ingraining wellbeing in the organization. When looking at employee reward and promotion, it is important for an organization to consider its values and whether the employee in question is "walking the walk". Employees should be treated in a fair and consistent manner and organizations should think carefully before rewarding undesirable behaviors and practices that undermine the organization's values. Many law firms have now changed their performance bonuses from being solely based on billable hours to include other performance criteria. This can help organizations to ensure that they are not rewarding negative behaviors such as over-working.

Billable hour targets

For those working in private practice, billable hours targets are common in most organizations. The pressure of working in a target-driven industry can be difficult, with many lawyers citing billable hours targets as a contributing factor of their stress at work. Many firms have moved away from formal individual billable hours targets and have switched to a team- or department-based approach which does, to a certain extent, help alleviate some of the pressure. In circumstances where billable hour targets cannot be removed, organizations should ensure that their billable hours targets are realistic, reviewed regularly, and that their employees are sufficiently supported in meeting their targets. It may also be helpful for firms to publicize their billable hours targets so that individuals looking to join a firm know at the outset what would be expected of them should they join. Where bonuses are linked to billable hours, they should not be based on unrealistic targets and should ideally include other metrics, in addition to billable hours, such as collaboration and demonstrating pro-social behaviors.

Work allocation

Transparency around work allocation is very important, particularly for those at the junior end of the profession who are more likely to receive work through many different avenues. More recently, several larger law firms have appointed work allocation/resourcing managers whilst others use online work status tools to measure work levels to ensure lawyers are not being over-burdened. Managers should be leading by example to ensure that they are monitoring workloads to allocate work in an appropriate way, taking into account the workload already allocated to individuals. By checking in with employees regularly, managers can ensure that work levels are manageable and, as a result, hopefully create a more open culture where those who are struggling feel able to ask for support.

The future

It is clear that negative stress and mental ill health continue to adversely affect the legal profession as a whole. There is real value in investing time and resource to improve employees' wellbeing and mental health. The profession as a whole needs to change and law firms need to be confident in challenging their clients on their expectations. Lawyers are keen to over-deliver and over-promise and that should not come at the expense of their wellbeing.

Whilst this chapter focuses on the negative results of the JLD's surveys and preparation of the best practice guidance, it is clear that times are certainly changing and that employers are now putting employee well-being onto their agendas. Law is a very rewarding and enjoyable career, and many lawyers thrive on the pressure of the nature of how lawyers work. It is when that pressure turns into negative stress, which junior lawyers are not equipped to deal with, that it causes problems. There is certainly a balance required in sharing the reality of working in the law through the results of the JLD's surveys and deterring aspiring lawyers from wanting to join our wonderful profession.

The legal profession is at risk of losing some of its best talent if employers do not begin to embrace their employees' wellbeing as a key asset for their business. By supporting employees and providing them with the necessary tools and resources to succeed, employers can reduce absence, lessen the risk of mistakes, increase productivity, and create organizations that attract and retain the best talent.

References

1. Defined as being under too much emotional or mental pressure.
2. Defined as experiencing a mental health problem/mental ill health (whether formally diagnosed or not).
3. Junior Lawyers Division – resilience and wellbeing survey results report 2017: https://communities.lawsociety.org.uk/Uploads/g/x/g/jld-resilience-and-wellbeing-survey-report-2017.pdf; Junior Lawyers Division – resilience and wellbeing survey results report 2018: https://communities.lawsociety.org.uk/Uploads/p/d/i/jld-resilience-and-wellbeing-survey-report-2018.pdf; and Junior Lawyers Division – wellbeing survey results report 2019: https://communities.lawsociety.org.uk/Uploads/b/y/k/resilience-wellbeing-survey-report-2019.pdf.
4. The Law Society's Annual Statistics Report 2018: www.lawsociety.org.uk/support-services/research-trends/documents/annual-statistics-report-2018/
5. Ibid.
6. Vulnerable by virtue of age, mental, or physical health difficulty, as a result of being in custody through lack of capacity, through experience of trauma, or who are vulnerable for any other reason.
7. *The Times* – Stopping a mental health crisis before it begins, Edward Fennell: www.thetimes.co.uk/article/stopping-a-mental-health-crisis-before-it-begins-zz7t77x6k
8. The Brief – *The Times* – Firms dice with negligence claims by overworking young lawyers http://nuk-tnl-deck-email.s3.amazonaws.com/11/d77c703536718b95308130ff2e5cf9ee.html
9. Junior Lawyers Division – Supporting resilience and wellbeing in the workplace: guidance for best practice: https://communities.lawsociety.org.uk/Uploads/d/d/n/Supporting-resilience-and-wellbeing-in-the-workplace.PDF
10. Junior Lawyers Division – Supporting wellbeing in the workplace: guidance for best practice: www.lawsociety.org.uk/support-services/documents/supporting-wellbeing-in-the-workplace-guidance-october-2019

Chapter 8:
Anxiety in the legal community – a study of junior lawyers, legal practice, and legal education

By Professor Richard Collier FAcSS, FRSA, Newcastle Law School, Newcastle University, UK

Introduction

In recent years legal professions internationally have experienced growing concern about the wellbeing and mental health of lawyers. The UK legal community is no exception, and heightened interest in the topic is reflected across an array of practical and policy initiatives, reports, research studies, articles and books, as well as substantial media coverage. This legal wellness literature in the UK, as elsewhere, tends to focus primarily on lawyer wellbeing across the diverse areas of legal professional practice, law students within legal education and training and, recently, if to a lesser degree, legal academics. This chapter addresses one issue receiving particular attention in these debates – the wellbeing of *junior lawyers*. The structure is as follows. First, we set the scene by briefly reviewing developments around wellbeing in the twin contexts of legal professional practice and university legal education. Second, we'll summarize the findings of a recent study into junior lawyer wellbeing and anxiety funded by the charity Anxiety UK (see further below).[1] Finally, thoughts are given on what might "connect" discussions of junior lawyer and law student wellbeing with regard to my central concern – understanding of anxiety, wellbeing, and mental health across the legal community.[2] There is no one unitary "wellbeing problem" in these diverse sectors.[3] Nonetheless, and seeking to move "beyond silos" in this wellbeing debate, contemporary research across discrete legal communities can learn much from a deeper consideration of what may be shared in the law and what these discussions of wellbeing might tell us about the changing nature of legal professionalism itself.[4]

Setting the scene – lawyer and law student wellbeing and mental health

A growing body of work across the UK legal profession, as noted above, is highlighting the scale of problems that exist around lawyer wellbeing and mental health. Recent studies and policy developments by Law Societies,[5] bodies representing junior lawyers,[6] at the Bar,[7] and on the part of regulators such as the Solicitors Regulation Authority (SRA),[8] alongside an array of initiatives across law firms[9] and other reports[10] each suggest wellbeing is an issue of increasing concern in the profession. In UK university law schools, meanwhile, there is heightened interest in law student wellness prompted, in part, by the high numbers of law students self-disclosing a wide range of mental health problems, not least in relation to experiences of anxiety.[11] A vortex of forces appear to be heightening pressures on university students and, perhaps especially, those on vocational courses such as law.[12] In this context many UK university law schools are seeking to review and bolster the support offered to their students via the introduction of a host of wellbeing activities and related developments.

Legal scholarship in the UK, meanwhile, is also increasingly exploring issues of direct relevance to understandings of wellbeing and anxiety; what contribution, for example, can an engagement with law and emotion,[13] the principles of positive psychology, insights of self-determination theory and therapeutic jurisprudence make to better understanding the management of subjective wellbeing in legal practice and education? There is a growing focus in legal studies internationally on the law curriculum and "intentional design" for wellbeing,[14] the place of resilience within university legal education,[15] the nature of the transition from education and training to legal practice;[16] on the ethical obligations that providers of legal education have to "educate for wellbeing" and how law school teaching practices and cultures can impact in deleterious ways on law students;[17] and in relation to debates around emotional competency and what it might mean to be "fit for law".[18]

The study: anxiety and wellbeing among junior lawyers – selected findings and themes

The *2019 Junior Lawyers Division (JLD) Resilience and Wellbeing Survey*, alongside earlier research, certainly paints a troubling picture of levels of negative stress and mental ill health experienced by junior lawyers. It highlights a range of issues for the profession, including the importance of fostering healthy working environments in which junior lawyers can develop and thrive and ensuring lawyers are not left feeling unsupported in the early years of their career. This chapter seeks to flesh out the findings of these 2019, 2018, and 2017 *JLD* surveys of wellbeing and resilience by interrogating the lived experiences of junior lawyers, defined for the purposes of the study as trainee solicitors, paralegals, and solicitors with up to five years' post-qualification experience (PQE). The funding supported a focused empirical study based on in-depth semi-structured interviews (each taking around one hour) with 12 practicing solicitors across a range of law firms and diverse areas of legal practice in the UK. Core research questions included (and were not confined to):

- How is anxiety experienced and understood in relation to these debates around lawyer wellbeing?
- What practices and cultures in the workplace and legal education are linked to particular anxiety difficulties for junior lawyers?
- What organizational attempts are being made to promote improved awareness of anxiety and support staff who do face difficulties?
- What is, and might be, the role of law firms and professional-related bodies, such as (amongst others) the charity LawCare, Law Societies, and the SRA in this area?

In keeping with the qualitative tradition, the interview method was seen as ideal in eliciting information mapping perceptions of how legal practice, organizational culture, and structures link to experiences of anxiety. With regard to methodology, this self-selected sample has, as is widely recognized in relation to projects of this kind, the potential impact to skew opinion towards negative interpretations of wellbeing; the criticism being that many respondents may be individuals who are already disaffected to varying degrees and who have experienced past or ongoing problems around anxiety. Contra to such a view, these are the very individuals whose insights are invaluable in developing deeper appreciation and understanding of the problem, adding texture and complexity to quantitative surveys. Of the 12 interviewees it is to be noted that 11 were female and one male (see below), a split that mirrors the marked gender disparity evident in other studies of lawyer wellbeing.

Interviewees viewed the factors contributing to poor junior lawyer wellbeing as varying across legal practice. The distinctive pressures associated with client demands, for example, well-documented concerns around competitive workplace cultures, issues of vicarious/secondary trauma and the impact of the organization and form of billing of legal work were seen as more acute in some areas of law than others (with marked differences in understandings of stress and workplace collegiality in the contexts of large corporate firms, "High Street" practice, in-house and law center and legal aid work). Notwithstanding such diversity, however, several recurring themes emerged.

The need to challenge stigma around anxiety and "speak out"

Notwithstanding what was acknowledged to be a greater visibility of wellbeing and mental health agendas, there was seen to remain a pervasive cultural stigma around disclosing anxiety problems in law. All interviewees saw it as essential that understandings of anxiety be separated from ideas of weakness. In particular, and mirroring the *JLD* studies above, distinctive pressures could be faced by lawyers early in their career which made it difficult to speak out about problems; a concern around the possible implications of disclosing difficulties, the need to be seen as "bullet-proof" in coping with work demands when starting out and so forth.

Law as an "anxiety-inducing" profession – competition and the route to qualification

Interviewees routinely depicted the process of qualification as a lawyer as highly anxiety-inducing. The experiences of legal practice, education, and training were each viewed as being marked by competitive cultures that fostered a sense of anxiety around what it means to be "getting on" and, ultimately, around what it meant to be a successful lawyer. The process of qualifying as a "proper" lawyer – which included, for some, the move from being a paralegal to trainee solicitor – was itself described as an anxiety-inducing transition; one that entailed "jumping through hoops, passing exams, applying for training contracts… and always worrying if there will… be a job". Qualifying as a lawyer, and the shift from legal education to employment, was viewed through a lens of anxiety in which a sense of "never knowing if you'll get there" was bound up with a belief that anxiety had, more generally, become commonplace in this professional world.[19] Significantly for these junior lawyers, this linked not just to specific aspects of the work (see below) but also a constant need to prove oneself in a context of considerable precarity and uncertainty around professional futures within the sector.

Legal education and the role of university law schools

Looking to connections between law school and legal practice discussed above, meanwhile, interviewees questioned the role of university law schools and providers of vocational education and training in supporting junior lawyer wellbeing (with two-thirds of these interviewees holding a qualifying law degree). Reflecting on their own experiences of law school, none had encountered dedicated sessions on wellbeing and anxiety as part of the law curriculum. It was also recognized, however, that this position may have changed in recent years in the light of growing concern about the wellbeing and mental health of UK university students considered above. Interviewees questioned, in particular, if the traditional university law degree could have better supported the wellbeing of students and prepare those who do enter practice. This was linked to issues of core competency requirements and questions about the place of emotion in legal education and professional practice. Further reference was made to the potential of clinical components, developing new approaches to dispute resolution and the need for the profession to recognize the value of diverse styles of communication. Two interviewees explicitly referred to the implications of poor junior lawyer wellbeing for regulators such as the SRA, Bar Standards Board, and the Chartered Institute for Legal Executives (CILEx) Regulation, exemplified by recent cases involving junior lawyers before the Solicitor's Disciplinary Tribunal.

The reasons why so many law students appear to be experiencing problems in relation to anxiety were described as multiple, encompassing concerns about, for example, funding and financial stress around repaying Legal Practice Course (LPC) loans (with no clear view expressed as to whether the proposed two-stage SQE (Solicitors Qualifying Exam) will address concerns); uncertainty around future careers; the need to "do well"; the nature of the law curriculum and assessment processes, as above; a lack of support around the transition not just to but also *from* university; and broader issues relating to concerns around friendship/peer relationships and structural, economic, and cultural shifts impacting on the experiences of students within an increasingly marketized Higher Education sector. Interviewees questioned whether law schools might better highlight the ways in which a greater focus on *intrinsic motivation* in career choices is linked to positive wellbeing; and if, as part of an ethical obligation to students and developing this wellbeing agenda, law schools and providers of legal education and training should challenge a dominant employability narrative and send more realistic messages about the nature of the legal labor market awaiting their students.

Work–life balance, long hours, and client demands

Mapping to the *JLD* studies above, all interviewees suggested that concerns around high workload and poor work–life balance were common across the profession but that junior lawyers could face distinctive pressures in ways that had implications for wellbeing. Particular problems were linked to lack of flexibility in working arrangements and deadlines in relation to partner and client demands; and, especially in certain areas and departments, the requirement to work unpredictable and frequently long hours. Other concerns included the potentially "double-edged" impact of new technologies and remote working; low decision latitude and lack of control over work and issues around pay, recognition, reward and fairness.

It is important to note, however, that these concerns were also seen as part of the "package deal" a junior lawyer would buy into in the route to becoming a lawyer; a relationship between "work" and "life" that would be likely to continue into their legal careers.[20] It was also recognized, by all interviewees, that a successful career in law could, for some at least, if certainly not all, bring relatively high financial rewards and social status.

"Perhaps it's just the people we are?" Reflecting on anxiety

Linking to well-established themes in the international literature on both law student and lawyer wellbeing, interviewees reflected on the distinctive "personality attributes" of those who enter law. Frequent reference was made to the idea that many lawyers were "insecure overachievers" with marked tendencies towards perfectionism and "imposter syndrome". The latter was seen as a particular issue for those starting out on a career in law, where highly demanding self-expectations could be bound up with the fear of making a mistake in ways that led to constant self-vigilance and, with it, a sense of anxiety. It was suggested in three interviews that law firms actively seek to select people driven by a need to exceed expectations, characteristics fostered by an educational system and work environment marked by intense competition around credentialization, appointment, and promotion. The interviews also suggest that competition and tendencies to perfectionism were bound up with a sense of living up to what was expected by others: "I mean, I'm so lucky to have a training contract, I keep thinking I should be grateful".

Understandings of anxiety and self-care

Just as mental health is a broad term, encompassing a wide range of diagnostic categories and subjective experiences, frequent reference was also made to how there was no "one" experience of anxiety. Interviewees interpreted the term in a variety of ways, subsumed within a wide set of concerns around wellbeing and mental health in the profession. Particular reference was made to intense/distressing feelings of worry in relation to work demands; low mood; worries about lack of focus/concentration; fatigue and feeling physically sick, panic attacks, chest pains, irritability, insomnia/disrupted sleep and emotional exhaustion; problems relating to vicarious/secondary trauma; detachment, social anxiety and feelings of low accomplishment and more general concerns around being ineffective at work.

The self-care strategies seen in the interviews as personally helpful in dealing with anxiety included exercise, connecting with others, taking time out and regular breaks, undertaking courses and utilizing the wellbeing resources that were available (with frequent mention made of mindfulness), addressing poor sleep, improving diet, and staying hydrated. Anecdotally, mention was also made of other common mechanisms amongst junior lawyers in dealing with anxiety and work demands, including alcohol consumption, self-medication, and tendencies to overwork/work long hours to complete tasks.

What works – and what doesn't – management and the limits of resilience

The interviews strongly support the *JLD Resilience and Wellbeing Surveys* in highlighting the pivotal importance of management and the need for adequate line manager training in dealing with mental health matters relating to anxiety. Repeated reference was made to the need for managers to develop a better understanding of the specific experiences and circumstances of trainees and early career lawyers, to be approachable and have regular check-ins where possible. This connects to broader concerns about the desirability of promoting mental health literacy in the profession, again mapping to the *JLD* themes around the need for support and education. Additional examples of desirable practice included the showcasing of lawyers, especially senior employees such as law firm partners, who had experienced periods of mental ill health; visible signs of law firm commitment to improved wellbeing, such as the signing of Workplace Wellbeing Charters and, related to this, the role-modelling of openness around mental health difficulties, including anxiety; the need to embed wellbeing-congruent behavior across the firm; and the introduction of training and wellbeing workshops and accessible and approachable mental health first aiders (MHFAs), wellbeing mentors and "champions" as prominent features of law firm culture.

It is important to recognize, however, that interviewees also questioned an approach to wellbeing that was seen to encourage individual lawyers to do something about their *own* wellbeing without addressing the broader *causes* of distress. Several challenged, for example, the idea that lawyers should just "become resilient", suggesting that this could slide into self-blame and a furthering of distress; and that it could also legitimate in law firms a "ticking the box" approach rather than seeking to bring about more substantive change in the profession. Whilst recognizing the responsibility of individual lawyers to attend to their own wellbeing and be responsible, and noting the limitations of what law firms could do to address problems, it was also seen as imperative that the profession did not lose sight of the structures and cultures productive of experiences of poor wellbeing in the first place; and, with it, the need for a culture of cooperation between employer and employee.

Concluding remarks

The research suggests pressures and concerns relating to anxiety on the part of these junior lawyers are shaped not only by the stage of life course and career but also a particular understanding of legal professionalism that shapes the distinctive practice areas in which lawyers work. All interviewees recognized that high levels of job stress could coincide with high levels of job satisfaction; frequent reference was made to the joys, rewards, pleasures, and challenges that were also part of developing a career as a lawyer. Several provided accounts of good practice in law firms including instances of practical support provided by managers and peers. Yet the idea that poor wellbeing should be accepted as "just how things are" in law was strongly challenged; as was the assumption that the "bottom-line" of client satisfaction would inevitably ensure working practices harmful to health "goes with the territory" of being a lawyer. This supports other research in suggesting that some specific aspects of legal culture have an important role in sustaining the paradox of satisfied lawyers who are under working conditions that may be conducive to stress, including experiences of anxiety.

A growing body of literature suggests the wellbeing and mental health of lawyers should be seen as a core business issues for law firms, with clear and evidenced benefits in terms of costs, retention, and recruitment. Generational and demographic changes in the profession, meanwhile, suggest problems in this area will not go away. This research supports the view that there may be a generational shift taking place in the legal profession, reflected in the greater willingness on the part of Millennials to be open about mental health issues; and, looking to the *JLD Wellbeing and Resilience Surveys*, above, this is itself now a key factor driving wellbeing debates in law. Several interviewees observed how networks were forming and conversations taking place about mental health in the legal community, including an openness around anxiety, that would have been difficult to imagine even ten years ago;

and that this discussion of wellbeing is itself closely interlinked to issues of equality, diversity, and inclusion in the profession. All, for example, felt there to be marked differences in men's and women's experiences of, and willingness to speak about, poor mental health; and that engaging senior men was central to advancing this agenda (mapping to themes in the Law Society's 2019 report and toolkit, *Male Champions for Change*). Several highlighted how their own wellbeing and anxiety directly linked to experiences of uncivil workplaces, with examples provided of the gendered nature of legal cultures and practices, including discussion of harassment and discrimination.[21] Two interviewees referred to the specificity of their own experiences as BAME lawyers. One noted how lawyers with disabilities could face particular difficulties in legal workplaces where ableism is endemic. Attempts to develop new ways of working in law, meanwhile, and to challenge traditional models around billing, work culture, allocation and organizational structures, were similarly framed as wellbeing and quality of life issues.

In conclusion, this study of junior lawyers' own life experiences strongly supports the 2018 *JLD Guidance for Best Practice* in drawing attention to the "three core pillars" of addressing (a) workplace *culture* in ways that would help combat problems around stress and anxiety-related depression in the legal profession; (b) the *support* provided to junior lawyers, including encouraging lawyers who are experiencing problems to self-disclose and seek help; and (c) the need for appropriate *education and training* in mental health literacy. It additionally draws attention to the role that legal education and training can play in the perpetuation of these problems. The themes discussed above suggest organizational responses to problems should themselves be multi-dimensional and cut across the legal community, including the interface between legal practice and legal education and training.

This debate is raising significant questions about how law firms respond to evidence of a far greater awareness of the complex interactions between mental health and the workplace; of the need to work in more effective, efficient, and safer ways; and, looking to generational shifts in attitudes, the greater willingness of younger lawyers to be open about mental health issues. In the context of a rapidly changing legal profession and marketplace for legal services, listening to the voices of lawyers suggests taking wellbeing seriously is becoming a key part of what it now means to be a good employer and provide a first-class service to clients.

References

1. R. Collier (2019) *Anxiety and Wellbeing Amongst Junior Lawyers: A Research Study*, available at: www.ncl.ac.uk/media/wwwnclacuk/newcastleuniversitylawschool/files/RC%20Briefing%20Digital.pdf.
2. Discussion focuses primarily on UK university law schools and the academic stage of legal education. It is important to note, however, that providers of vocational legal education are similarly facing growing concerns around wellbeing and mental health amongst law students.
3. R. Collier (2016) "Wellbeing in the Legal Profession: reflections on recent developments (or, what do we talk about when we talk about wellbeing?)" 23(1) *International Journal of the Legal Profession* 41-60.
4. These themes are explored in more depth in R. Collier (in press, 2020) "Reflections on the UK Experience of Legal Academic Wellbeing and the Legal Professions: Moving Across Silos?" in J. Chan, P. Vines and M. Legg (eds) *The Impact of Technology and Innovation on the wellbeing of Lawyers*, Intersentia.
5. For example, Law Society (2014) *Solicitors' Health and Well-being: The Law Society's PC Holders Survey 2014*, London, The Law Society.
6. Law Society (2018) *Supporting Resilience and Wellbeing in the Workplace: Guidance for best Practice*, London, The Law Society; Law Society (2019) *Resilience and Wellbeing Survey Report: Junior Lawyers Division* London, The Law Society, available at: https://communities.lawsociety.org.uk/Uploads/b/y/k/resilience-wellbeing-survey-report-2019.pdf
7. *Positive, Wellbeing at the Bar: A Resilience Framework Assessment (RFA) by Positive*, London, Positive, 2015, available at: www.barcouncil.org.uk/media/348371/wellbeing_at_the_bar_report_april_2015__final_.pdf
8. Solicitor's Regulation Authority (SRA), "Your Health, Your Career", available at: www.sra.org.uk/solicitors/resources/your-health-your-career/
9. Note, for example, the *Mindful Business Charter* available at https://home.barclays/content/dam/home-barclays/documents/who-we-are/Mindful%20Business%20Charter%202018.pdf
10. *The Bellwether Report 2019: Stress in the Legal Professions – Problematic or Inevitable?* available at: www.lexisnexis.co.uk/research-and-reports/stress-in-the-legal-profession-problematic-or-inevitable.html
11. See, for example, C. Baksi, "Help is at hand for students struggling with Mental health", *The Times Brief: Student Law Week*, 19 February 2018 www.thetimesbrief.co.uk/users/39765-catherine-baksi/posts/30357-help-is-at-hand-for-students-struggling-with-mental-health
12. M. Thornton (2016) "The Case of Law Student Wellbeing: A Neoliberal Conundrum" 58(2) *Australian Universities Review* 42-50.
13. E. Jones (2019) *Emotions in the Law School: Transforming Legal education through the Passions*, London, Routledge.
14. Legal Education Research Network/IALS, Positive Psychology Workshop. *Intentional Education Design for Well-being*, 2 May 2019, http://ials.sas.ac.uk/events/event/19653

15. L. Bleasdale and S. Humphries, *Undergraduate Resilience Research Project*, Leeds University Institute for Teaching Excellence, Leeds, available at: file:///H:/2018%20Oct/LITEbleasdalehumphreys_fullreport_online.pdf.
16. Note, the work of the *City Mental Health Alliance* (CMHA): http://citymha.org.uk/wp-content/uploads/2018/07/CMHA-Thriving-at-Work-Guide-final-PDF.pdf
17. See further R. Field and C. Strevens (eds), *Educating for Well-Being in Law: Positive Professional Identities and Practice* (London, Routledge, 2019).
18. *Fit For Law: Emotional Competence and professional Resilience*, an online course produced by The Open University in collaboration with the charity LawCare: www.open.edu/openlearncreate/course/view.php?id=3476.
19. See further R. Martin (2018) *This Too Will Pass: Anxiety in a Professional World*, Newark: Trigger.
20. On the nature of this "deal" for fathers in the profession see R. Collier "Fatherhood, gender and the making of professional identity in large law firms: bringing men into the frame" 15(1) *International Journal of Law in Context*, 68.
21. See in particular International Bar Association (2019) *Us Too? Bullying and Harassment in the Legal profession* available at: www.ibanet.org/bullying-and-sexual-harassment.aspx

Chapter 9:
Supervision without stress

By Paul Bennett, solicitor and partner, Bennett Briegal LLP

Why is supervision stressful?

Supervising others is hard work; being supervised by someone is hard work. Every bookshop is full of books on managing people, online Ted Talks abound on managing people and on managing your manager. The volume of material highlights the challenge: everyone and every situation is unique and therefore what works for one person will be less effective or even counter-productive with another.

If you focus on the relationship, whether you are the supervisor or supervised individual, you have the capacity to reduce stress. My simple proposition is we all have an obligation to our colleagues to reduce stress levels.

The relationship is shown simply in Figure 1, which shows the two sets of wishes of the supervisor and the individual, which are naturally distinct.

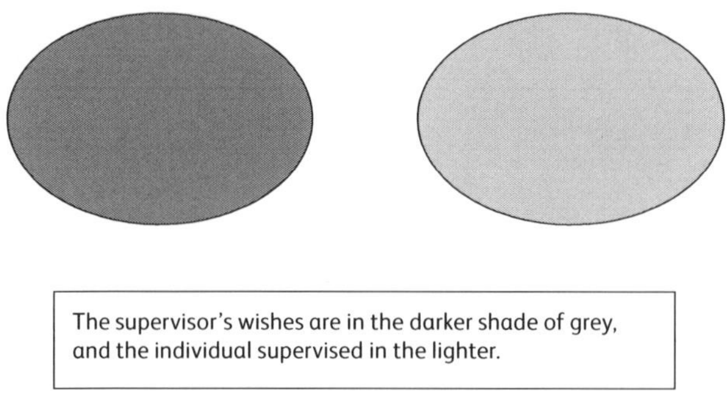

Figure 1 – Wishes of the supervisor and the person supervised.

Effective supervision that engages and inspires an individual should lead to Figure 2, where there is an overlap or joining of objectives.

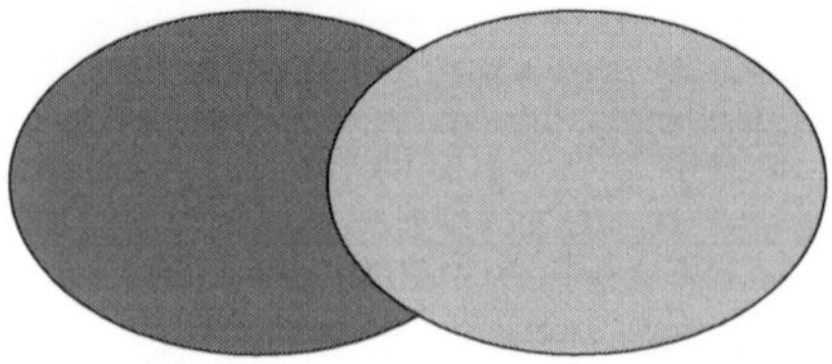

The supervisor's wishes are in the darker shade of grey, and the individual supervised in the lighter – an overlap should occur.

Figure 2 – Wishes of the supervisor and the person supervised when they work effectively together.

If you do not get the best from your team and they cannot reach your goals, you are likely to be experiencing the distance from the Figure 1 scenario and the relationship has to be improved to achieve Figure 2's combined objectives. However, if your supervisor is not getting the best from you, you will benefit if you can subtly help them realize what you need to be more effective. If someone is scared of a supervisor or fearful of embarrassment they will never achieve Figure 2.

The aim of this chapter

Something needs to change to make supervision less stressful in law firms. If you are a manager you should naturally want to get the best from your team. If you are a lawyer being supervised you want to go to work and not feel fear or the sense of being bullied.

Toxic cultures and stresses appear in many workplaces – chapter ten explores some of the extreme cases. This is not reflective of normality, but it is reflective of a growing awareness of the problems that poor management and poor supervision can cause.

Therefore, my aim is to challenge your thinking and get you to look at the supervision relationship differently – whether you are the senior or junior party, or whether in a larger firm you sit somewhere in the middle.

My first love story – an introduction

Do you remember the first time you were in love? The relationship suddenly meant everything to you and the other person involved. It was probably intense and at times confusing. Supervision is like that – intense and confusing.

Work-related stress across the board is widely perceived to be at an all-time high and law has gone from sleepwalking into a mental health crisis to a focus on wellbeing in the last couple of years.

Those who are in a supervisory relationship with you need to know you care, whether you are the supervisor, or the person being supervised. If your supervision approach has not changed in the last 25 years, even without knowing the details I can assure you it needs to evolve to improve.

"Is love the right analogy?" someone asked me recently when I talked them through their supervision challenges. My response was "Do those you supervise know you care about them? Do they know you have their back? Do they trust you? Do they believe you will undermine them with colleagues or clients?"

If they feel you will not support them, are always critical and do not care about their welfare, then you will not get the outcome you seek from staff. The undermining of those supervised I have often called "cheating on them" to take the love analogy to its limit.

As a profession we can no longer just assume those supervised have the same understanding of trust and confidence in us as law firm leaders as we intend. Therefore, my first love story focuses on four areas:

M Mistakes
F Feedback
L Leadership
S Supervision

In law firms we will encounter each of these issues to a degree. How you handle those issues will impact on your relationship. We will expand on the key words so they become themes in part two, but think first about how you deal with mistakes, feedback, and how you provide leadership and supervision will impact on the whole supervisory relationship. Do these basics well and you can go on to focus on the more challenging supervisory aspects, but do them poorly and you will have staff who underperform and are less productive than anticipated.

If you do not successfully complete these four basics aspects of supervision well, you will make your own life more difficult and you will cause stress to others. In part two below I explore the themes from the perspective of those who are supervised.

"My first love story" is a tool I developed to help the law firms I work with improve their supervisory relationships. Sport is full of lessons and analogies, but not everyone is into sport. Business is full of lessons, and authors such as Simon Sinek, whose seminal book *Start with why*, or Jim Collins, whose classic book *Good to Great*, remain popular years after publication because of a thirst to improve our management of businesses, people, and projects. The law-specific equivalents are probably written by those who are no longer in practice, so I have tried to distil down some themes to help my clients and I introduce those here. I ask clients to use the memory of their first love because, in a people business such as law, is it critical to get the relationships right or nothing else is as effective as it should be.

As lawyers, we train to deliver our legal knowledge to clients on the basis of the service they need. We develop legal knowledge and combine these with our advisory, drafting, and advocacy skills. Invariably we have spent years honing these skills to deliver the solutions that clients need without the client thinking about the years of skill development that has led to the position to advise clients. By contrast, how much time have you spent learning to supervise others effectively? How much management training have you undertaken to develop the skills involved? Most lawyers confess to me during training, coaching, or when under investigation by one of the legal regulators, that they have never really been trained for the supervisory role and have never focused much on the skills.

In terms of being supervised, how much time have you spent ensuring you are an effective member of the team? Do you focus on how you are supervised in comparison to your preferences or your personal wishes in terms of doing what you want?

Do you supervise others in a way that is effective, supportive, and allows lawyers to be open and transparent with their needs in terms of your supervision? I suggest all supervisors need to be trusted as a priority for supervision to work, so passing on stress or being inconsistent or moody will undermine everything else you do that is right.

If you are supervised by another and want to ensure your contribution is not detrimental to the wellbeing of others then this chapter is for you. It is also for everyone else in your team.

Supervision is a skill

Supervision is a skill and each time you use that skill you should be thinking about it and how you can improve that skill. If you drive a car you do not think, "I'm an amazing driver, I can definitely drive safely at 150 miles per hour in a built-up area next to my local school". Instead, you probably think, "It's a dark, wet, winter's evening and I can see children. I need to drive carefully." Such thinking is using your driving skills in the context of the environment.

If you focus on supervision in the same way, you will almost certainly supervise Martha and Nancy differently. They are different people, with different knowledge, skills and experiences. If you treat them the same you will not achieve the same outcome because each person is unique. If we assume Martha is a 15-year qualified solicitor who has experience of commercial transactions and is capable of leading a major project, and Nancy is a paralegal in her first role after university and doing the Legal Practice Course part-time, you will know the supervision should look different.

The same is true of two similarly experienced lawyers, because rarely will Harry and Harvinder have the same personality, skills, experience, and need for support. Each person you supervise or who supervises you needs to be assessed for their needs in context of that unique supervisory relationship.

Supervision is a relationship

All relationships need work, whether it is a marriage, friendship, team, or workplace.

Every relationship contains at least two personalities, and supervision in law firms is often a myriad of more complex relationships in the team. The dynamic can be challenging. I have worked successfully with colleagues who I did not particularly like or gel with, but I focused on being effective as a team unit. No doubt they would say "He was not my cup of tea" or similar about me. It is an artificial relationship, but it is one we have to make work.

Lots of business books draw on sport to exemplify management techniques, but in sport you typically have win, lose, or draw outcomes. In legal services, the outcomes are more varied – winning a claim, losing a claim, completing a deal, deciding not to complete a deal due to an intervening event, exploring legal options and risks to name just the core outcomes I see most weeks.

Ask yourself some tough questions if you want your workplace relationships to be strong. I encourage you to write down and reflect on the following:

- Why would anyone want to work for you?
- Why would anyone want you in their team?
- What do you do to work at your supervision relationships?
- If you are being supervised, do you work with your supervisor to ensure they get the best out of you?
- What quality do you add in the context of your team?

Sometimes the answers might be uncomfortable. In the past I accept I have been so bored and uninspired by colleagues in law firms due to their poor leadership that I have probably noted their faults and not focused on my own.

Everything in this chapter starts with managing yourself effectively, whether you are the supervisor or the supervised employee. Someone committed to the relationship would help colleagues, including supervisors who are out of their depth to perform. As a profession we have built cultures of looking out for our colleagues, and with poor leader colleagues in my past I have tried to steer them (once I have realized they are struggling) to ensure they get support. Supervision is about the relationship, so it is a two-way street.

Set the standards

Who sets the standards in your team? You. If you are junior you can still set the standards regarding how you conduct yourself.

Lead by example and make sure the standards reflect your expectation on others. If you focus on client care and the client experience, others in the team will do the same. This is as true of a junior member of the team giving great client service as it is on anyone in a leadership position.

Once one person sets a high standard in one aspect of legal practice, others will naturally see the standard and start to use it as a benchmark. This is a double-edged sword because if you are disengaged, disinterested, and going through the motions, that will impact on the relationship. By contrast, if you set high standards, others will try to elevate their work to those high standards. Again, this is true of junior lawyers, who can influence the team around them and their line managers.

Supervisor's perspective

In setting the standards you can raise them subtly by how you engage and encourage your team. If you do not discuss the difficult issues and the weaknesses, then those you supervise will be unaware of your expectations. You can start by setting the standards, wooing them and setting your standard as their benchmark. I use the word "wooing" deliberately – you need them to want it, so you need them to be interested in you and the standards you are setting. You start by showing, then explaining (not undermining or knocking their confidence) and you build their skills by supporting them in achieving the standards you are setting.

You will not woo your team if you are inconsistent, unreasonable, and cannot be trusted to look out for them. If your team are struggling with your moods or inconsistent approach they cannot change that – you can.

Small steps can help you be consistent and to build trust. Write down your core requirements.

Be trusted

If you are going to lead a successful team, then being trusted is essential. There are no excuses – however dull or obnoxious the colleague – and we have all experienced plenty of those in law firms, you need to earn their respect. It does not come from status, experience, or client excellence – it comes from the fact they can trust you. Senior or junior, you need to be trustworthy.

As a team member and someone being supervised, do your colleagues trust you? Does your supervisor know you will ask for help when you need it? Do you try and solve problems or put up barriers and give yourself excuses? Do you showcase that you have the ability to stretch your knowledge and skills in a way that protects clients and the firm appropriately?

Are you fair and honest to those you work with? If you have said something will happen, do they know it will, or do they need to check, double-check, and remind you before you finally commit and complete the task in hand?

Do you treat everyone equally and fairly? Do you have a favorite person in your team as a supervisor? How does that impact on the team dynamic and other people? Each person in every team needs to be accountable for their colleagues' level of trust in them.

Beware of the micromanager

I was discussing micromanaging staff with someone recently and they said, "When I do anything, I do it right!" The implication was others did it wrong, so I asked them if the legal work they did only ever had one solution they said "No". Slowly I built a picture around why their solution was so vital to them when other lawyers acting for the other party might think they knew the best solution available. The point suddenly hit home that their micromanaging of their team stemmed from their insecurity that others might question how they preferred to work.

We all have our preferences and our own style, and sometimes we have to accept that other people's style is not to our liking, but it works for them. Micromanaging is often a sign of insecurity, but it also has a devastating impact on junior staff because they do not get the chance to grow and show their full abilities and it undermines their confidence.

Ask yourself, "Why would anyone wish to be micromanaged by me?" Another micromanager said to me, "It's my reputation and I do not like their style so that justifies my approach," to which I replied, "Why has no one worked for you for more than a year?" It was uncomfortable but they slowly learnt to be a better supervisor, starting with guiding their current junior on their style wishes. We explored how exhausting the turnover of staff was for that individual and how they could set the standards without micromanaging.

The question is therefore not would I have done that, but rather does it achieve the client's objectives?

Every person I have hired in law firms over the last 12 years has been better than me at something. A successful entrepreneur said to me, only hire people who are better than you at something, and it struck a chord. If you hire people or take on a team and spot an individual's core skills and talents and use it whilst coaching them on their weakness and your preferences, it is far more effective than micromanaging.

The basic process

Nothing I have written above is ground-breaking or radical, it is incredibly basic. As a supervisor myself I have not always got it right so if you have a day when you get it wrong, be open and focus on rebuilding the trust. In 2009 I created a diagram to explain the relationship to a client. It is very basic but has stood the test of time, and whilst I might play with the words used it uses all the themes identified above – be trusted, give feedback in a positive and constructive manner, and handle mistakes and fault finding in the right way.

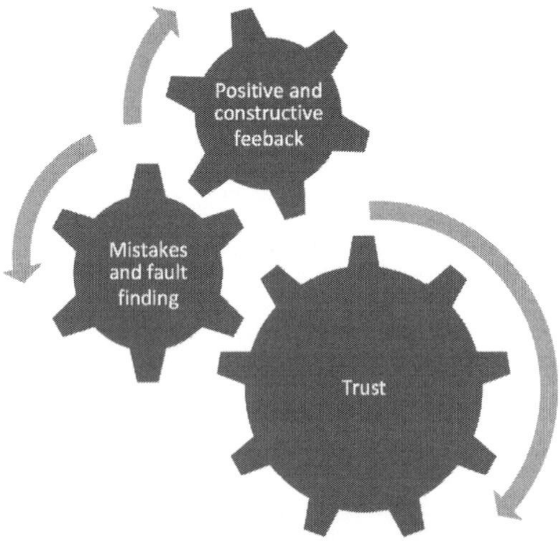

Figure 3: The fully-functioning relationship.

I find that a visual outline helps some people grasp the concepts. It looks so simple but if you fail to get the cogs working together then, unsurprisingly, things go awry.

My first love story – part 2

You should by now be thinking: how can I be a better supervisor and avoid causing unnecessary stress to my team? Or how can I help my supervisor get the best out of me?
The expanded version of my first love story is this:

M Mistakes – Dealing with mistakes in a manner that builds confidence.
F Feedback – Giving constructive feedback and building trust with those you supervise.
L Leadership – Leading by example.
S Supervision – Supervise and do not micromanage.

The issue of mistakes is critical to trust and confidence next time work is undertaken. If, as a supervised lawyer, you hide your mistakes, you will undermine a supervisor's confidence in you. It is not just the supervisor who needs to build trust, but all staff.

Feedback is a two-way street. Try, "I was not sure if you wanted X or Y: I have shown both options so you can choose," or "Before I complete the work, did you want X or Y? I am not sure, and I want to deliver exactly what you need me to." Both are subtle ways of exploring the lack of clarity in directions given to you by a supervisor.

Leadership is about exemplifying what you expect. As a junior in a team you may not be in a leadership position, but it is fair for law firms to expect you to demonstrate leadership in terms of how you treat others, how you ask for support, and how you interact with your supervisors so they know how you prefer to interact with others to feel most able to work effectively in a team.

If you have a concern, think about resetting to the basics explored above and in Figure 3. Ask yourself, "Can I contribute to effective supervision by asking questions? By trying something new? By willing to be challenged?"

It is about constantly managing yourself – senior or junior – to work on your supervision skills and display those skills for the benefit of those you work with.

Stress

Law is a stressful profession, but that does not mean we should be stressed all the time. We all have a duty to look after ourselves and look after each other.

Supervision without stress is about taking responsibility for yourself, your impact on others, and for supporting others. You do that by focusing on the skills and being someone that other people want to work for, rather than by being the "difficult" member of the team.

Junior or senior, if you are involved in supervision you need to ensure that the overlap of objectives set out in Figure 2 applies. It's not about you and your wishes or needs, but those combined goals.

The thrill of pre-trial pressure or big deal is part and parcel of healthy stress, and if your team is functioning right they will be boosted by those challenges. If you get supervision wrong it can crush individuals, so we all have an obligation to work on our skills. Not all stress is therefore bad, but if it's too much, reset to the basics explored here to ensure your supervision is without stress on others.

Chapter 10: Lawyers' mental health, the Solicitors Disciplinary Tribunal, and the courts

By Paul Bennett, solicitor, Bennett Briegal LLP

Introduction

As society's understanding of mental health has developed over the last ten to 15 years, professions have started to evolve. It is my personal view that the evolution is too slow, and we are letting down society by not reflecting it more accurately. However, the cases that often capture the eye may not be the best examples of systemic failings, which in turn slows further the evolution, causing the wellbeing progress to lose considerable momentum.

Issues of sexuality, race, religion, gender, and physical disability are far higher up the agenda for regulators generally than mental health and wellbeing.

In this chapter I cite contrasting cases I have been involved in, regarding a doctor and a solicitor. The doctor's misconduct almost led to a patient's death; the solicitor's conduct led to a delayed payment of compensation. It is a good contrast to pose the question: Have the Tribunals and Courts misunderstood mental health?

The purposeful approach of the Courts

The Courts have a well-rehearsed starting point in most professional disciplinary cases across the professions. It stems from the seminal judgment in *Bolton v. Law Society* (1994) 1 WLR 512, CA at p.518:

> *"It is important that there should be full understanding of the reasons why the tribunal makes orders which might otherwise seem harsh… to maintain the reputation of the solicitors profession as one in which every member, of whatever standing, may be trusted to the ends of the earth."*

It is not therefore about the individual but about the collective reputation. An individual who commits misconduct is not treated as the primary purpose but the reputation of the profession is. Tribunals and

Courts routinely impose sanction that outside of the professions would seem harsh, but they do so to preserve the collective reputation.

The case law is not well established in the evolving mental health context, and for that reason it is likely we will continue to see an evolving landscape and may wish to reevaluate our professional rules.

The UK's Legal Services Act 2007

The UK's Legal Services Act 2007 (LSA2007) amended the Solicitors Act 1974 at Section 31, which now includes the option for the legal regulators (including the Solicitors Regulation Authority (SRA)) to introduce and utilize a set of Fitness to Practise rules. The SRA has failed to consult on or action this option.

The Solicitors Act 1974 reads in its amended form after the LSA2007:

> **"31 Rules as to professional practice, conduct and discipline:**
>
> (1) Without prejudice to any other provision of this Part the Society may make rule for regulating in respect of any matter the professional practice, conduct, *fitness to practise* and discipline of solicitors and for empowering the Society to take such action as may be appropriate to enable the Society to ascertain whether or not the provisions of rules made, or of any code or guidance issued, by the are being, or have been, complied with." [emphasis added in italics and by underlining]

For "Society" in the statute read the SRA, as under the LSA2007 the SRA was created and empowered to take over those functions from the Law Society of England and Wales.

Lawyers' wellbeing and mental health therefore is not a sufficient priority that the biggest regulator of legal services, the SRA, has felt inclined (in the 12 years since the LSA2007 created the SRA and it has been in force) to focus its attentions towards creating a Fitness to Practise regime. Such regimes have two purposes:

(1) To protect the public from unwell solicitors; and

(2) To help the profession manage the evolving mental health challenge.

The SRA is of course a baby regulator, being formed out of the LSA2007 itself, and it is maturing. Even a cynic such as I who deals with it daily can report it is a far better organization in 2020 than it was five years ago. In the next decade we should expect far more from the SRA to support the profession. Our expectations have been raised by improvements, and we occasionally despair at the missteps, but it is better now than it was, and we should encourage it to raise its own performance again.

Fitness to Practise

The Fitness to Practise position contrasts sharply with the healthcare professions in which the lead regulators all have Fitness to Practise regimes. It begs the question: what is so special about lawyers? In my view, nothing. We are not special. We are not unique. We should expect to be treated like every other profession. Unfortunately we are singled out for harsher expectations and sanctions.

If we want a truly diverse profession – one that is open to all and serves our communities and our businesses – then we want the profession to be open to all. My simple proposition to each and every reader is we should protect our colleagues' health and run a campaign to introduce a Fitness to Practise regime as it encourages diversity and will enhance public confidence in the profession by recognizing that lawyers must be professional – but they will, like we all do to some degree, make mistakes. How we handle those minor mistakes is key to them not being a major challenge or issue.

Dishonesty and mental health

A mental health condition should not permit a professional to act dishonestly. The case law I refer to below includes an element of dishonesty, sometimes centrally to the misconduct, but the impact of the mental health aspect raises the uncomfortable issue that judges and Tribunal panels need educating on the impact of mental health conditions in order to avoid adopting a one-size-fits-all approach to lawyers, which is unnecessary.

Case study: Daniel

Daniel was a doctor, a registrar, at one of the UK's leading hospitals. The pressures of work and the loss of his marriage with less access to his children took their toll on his mental health. One day he was administering an anesthetic to a patient undergoing surgery. Whilst the drug cabinet was open Daniel stole some of the drugs available to him due to his role, then injected them through his nose in an attempt to commit suicide. The circumstances were made worse as his patient was on a ventilator and Daniel, whilst unconscious, impacted on the ventilator, causing it to fail.

Daniel was treated by his colleagues and survived the attempted suicide. The patient made a full recovery. The swift actions of an outstanding medical team saved two lives that day.

The hospital dismissed Daniel for gross misconduct and reported matters to the GMC.

At his professional disciplinary hearing, Daniel admitted theft of the drug and endangering the life of his patient. The theft was dishonest, naturally, but the more serious impact was on patient safety and the risk to the public.

The Tribunal dealing with Daniel did not strike him off. Under the Fitness to Practise regime it suspended him from practise whilst his condition was treated, and his health recovered. It was an enlightened approach to mental health and misconduct.

When he was well enough, his misconduct led to a further Tribunal, and he was further suspended with a return date at a third disciplinary panel to prove he was fit to resume his career. Daniel was subject to 26 conditions to protect patients when he resumed his career, which were reduced over time.

Daniel is now a very successful doctor, healthy from a mental health perspective, with a condition in remission and a support network to allow him to seek help if the remission should cease. Daniel is able to continue his career.

Note: Daniel is not the doctor's real name. The material above is all public domain information. I acted in the case between 2009 and 2012 so the enlightened approach of the medical regulator is not new.

Case study: Sovani James

The case of Sovani James has attracted much publicity and comment. I acted in the case at both Solicitors Disciplinary Tribunal (SDT) as the only advocate and in High Court level, in which I was led in the hearing by Geoffrey Williams QC. As with Daniel's case, nothing I will say is not already in the public domain. The SDT decision reference is Case No. 11657-2017.

Ms James alleged she was bullied and therefore became mentally unwell. The SDT and later the High Court agreed this was the case. Her former employer's managers gave evidence this was not the case, so the exact position is disputed, but the factual findings of both hearings include findings of bullying and mental health challenges.

The SDT noted the mental health condition was diagnosed retrospectively but the physical impact had been clear and was accepted by both the SDT (and later the High Court) as including loss of hair, a regular (sometimes daily) state of tears, and obvious distress.

The allegations amounted to creation of false documents to avoid admitting a mistake to the firm because (it was said) of a fear of her supervisors.

The firm involved had requested a huge number of hours. The then CEO had demanded of staff they cancelled holidays, worked weekends, and focused on the fees ahead of a potential private equity investment.

The SDT agreed with my submission that the "toxic" workplace culture and the mental health condition amounted to an "exceptional circumstance", which merited deviating from the normal sanction in solicitor dishonesty cases: strike off.

At paragraph 61 of the SDT Judgment, the Tribunal stated:

> *"It was unusual for solicitors appearing before the Tribunal to use words such as "terrified" and "fear" in the context of the workplace. The use of those words gave an indication of the Respondent's vulnerability; small issues such as getting behind on a file had magnified to the extent that the consequences anticipated by the Respondent were dire and, in her own words, she felt as if she had a massive dark cloud hanging over her. The Respondent was vulnerable, isolated, dealing with difficult home circumstances, relatively young in terms of life experience, and in what she viewed as an environment that had become toxic to her. She had lost her confidence and felt that she was no good at a job that she had previously enjoyed. This was, in effect, a 'perfect storm' of circumstances."*

The SDT decision in effect was that the impact of health and the wider context was relevant; not simply the dishonesty itself.

Regrettably, the High Court overturned the decision on appeal. Lord Justice Flaux stated at paragraph 101:

> *"Inevitably, an assessment of the nature and extent of the dishonesty and the degree of culpability will involve an examination of what Ms Morris QC [a QC to a conjoined respondent] termed the "mind set" of the respondent, including whether the respondent is suffering from mental health issues and the workplace environment, as part of the overall balancing exercise. However, where the SDT has concluded that, notwithstanding any mental health issues or work or workplace related pressures, the respondent's misconduct was dishonest, the weight to be attached to those mental health and working environment issues in assessing the*

appropriate sanction will inevitably be less than is to be attached to other aspects of the dishonesty found, such as the length of time for which it was perpetrated, whether it was repeated and the harm which it caused, all of which must be of more significance. Certainly, it is difficult to see how in a case of dishonesty, as opposed to some lesser professional misconduct, the fact that the respondent suffered from stress and depression (whether alone or in combination with extreme pressure from the working environment) could without more amount to exceptional circumstances...."

Solicitors Regulation Authority v. James, MacGregor and Naylor [2018] EWHC 3058 (Admin)

The High Court had an exceptionally difficult task trying to hear three cases with dishonesty, workplace pressures, and mental health elements, which were unique and distinct in the case of *Naylor* and *MacGregor* from those issues in the *James* case. The impact has been to narrow the opportunity to successfully argue exceptional circumstances arguments before the SDT, and create a harsher environment for professionals.

The *MacGregor* and *Naylor* decisions both followed within a few short weeks the *James* case in the SDT, which was the first finding of exceptional circumstances in many years. The SRA appealed all three, as has been its policy for many years in exceptional circumstances cases. If the rules on sanction and Fitness to Practise were more flexible, then I suspect two of the three respondent solicitors would be back in the profession and successful today. The third case was weaker and thus it would have been lost whatever the regime. I am therefore arguing for decision-maker discretion.

The Court and the Regulators

The Court having to put speech marks around such a basic concept as "mind set" demonstrates the challenge that we as a profession still face. The rules and the decision-makers' thinking have yet to evolve sufficiently to catch up with wider society. Not everyone thinks it should evolve.

Perhaps the issues explored throughout this book should not impact on regulatory standards? As a profession, we have to assess, what do we really expect? What standards are the right standards for us? How do we encourage diversity and yet protect the public from misconduct?

Do the public expect doctors to be given significant leeway that should not apply to other professionals? Solicitors are treated differently, but nurses and pharmacists, for example, are more closely aligned with the position for doctors.

Conclusion

If we are serious about lawyer wellbeing and creating businesses that are good places to work, the debate of the last few years will have helped – but it is not the job of the High Court to enhance the regulatory framework; simply to apply it. The decision in the *James and others* case is an application of a regime that, in my view, is flawed. We should be helping the judiciary by giving them more knowledge of mental health and wellbeing and a wider set of options for sanction.

We should expect the SRA, the SDT, and even the widely-ridiculed Legal Services Board (the so-called super-regulator) to review the Fitness to Practise option. We should encourage them to work effectively to protect the public whilst promoting diversity to allow those who experience mental health episodes to be protected, supported, and to return to practice in appropriate cases.

The line is firmly drawn against solicitors at present – but surely that simply means the regulators need to assess if it has been drawn in the wrong place. I would encourage readers to lobby for a review of the mental health protections for lawyers and to encourage consideration of a Fitness to Practise regime.

Having acted for numerous professionals across perhaps ten or 12 regulators, the theme with those impacted by mental health is they are good people, good professionals, who made tragic decisions whilst unwell.

The current regime of mental health being minimized in regulatory decision-makers' thinking does not encourage diversity or serve the public interest as it encourages a profession that is not ready to be open, transparent, and inclusive on the issue of mental health. It is therefore time to try another approach.

Chapter 11: Wellbeing and the upskilling of lawyers – professional insights and practical applications

By James Pereira QC, FTB Chambers,[1] barrister and coach

Introduction

The map is not the territory.[2]

These words point to the difference between perception and reality – our experience of the world is not the world itself. Instead, our perception is an interpretation based on an internal map that we use to guide us through our life and its relationships, a map that is itself drawn from our experiences and learning.[3] Change the map, and you change the way you experience the world.

With a new map, broader horizons appear. Familiar places can then be explored with fresh perspectives. Life becomes richer and more resourceful. Choices that were previously hidden reveal themselves. Directions for growth open up, and future possibilities multiply.

Whether you are a lawyer or law firm employee concerned with professional development, or a professional engaged in evolving the legal profession through wellbeing interventions, you would do well to understand, and accept, this basic starting point. Doing so brings the realization that the skills that lawyers can develop to support their practices are far wider than traditional learning provides, or that the profession's outdated map is able clearly to see. With the right starting place, the right questions can be asked, and the right support obtained. The profession can then expand its vision.

The message is simple – supporting lawyer and law firm wellbeing enhances professional performance. It is important I explain what this means. My point is not that well lawyers make better lawyers. True though that may be, it is also rather trite, and apparently not enough of an incentive for the legal system to consistently value wellbeing as a necessary professional attribute. Nor am I advocating lawyer wellbeing as part of a wider social movement within the legal system. That movement is already well underway.[4] Instead, what I am saying is that appropriate and informed wellbeing interventions can deliver significant upskilling of lawyers within the context of mainstream legal practice. They can provide not merely a shield, but a sword – in fact, a whole range of effective weapons and tools for the lawyer's armory that can be drawn upon as required.

I offer this learning from a dual professional perspective, reflecting my dual professional role – one is that of a high-performing[5] lawyer who has faced severe wellbeing challenges of my own, eventually overcoming them to emerge a far stronger and more skillful lawyer as a result. The other is that of a professional systemic[6] coach who supports other lawyers and firms to grapple with and overcome their own wellbeing challenges, to upskill themselves, to redraw their own maps.

Failing to succeed

I start by giving some of my own back story of how I got to where I am. I have called it "failing to succeed". The verbal ambiguity, which is most unlawyerly, is entirely deliberate.

For most of my career as a barrister I have been fortunate to be ranked among the top practitioners of my specialist area. But until recent years, those professional highs had been matched by equally magnificent personal lows, and behind the glittering outward success was a dark inner struggle. Many a time I heard the siren call to simply give it all up. But three simple truths kept me in the game, eventually delivering me exactly where I needed to go.

Truth one: I deserve my success. I love working as a lawyer, I am not bad at it, I've worked hard to get to where I am, so why should I give up?

Truth two: only I am responsible for myself. My wellbeing and my happiness – just like the quality of my work – is my own responsibility, not anyone else's.

Truth three: nothing is written in stone. Specifically, the notion that professional success as a lawyer has to come at personal cost struck me as a dubious piece of received wisdom that needed to be questioned. It did not work for me and it was not working for others. There had to be a different, more resourceful, way to live, to work, and to serve clients. The map was not the territory. It seemed to me it was time to start drawing a better map.

I was called to the Bar in 1996. I had no family connections with the law. Both my parents are immigrants – one from India, the other from Ireland. I was fortunate to undertake training and then gain tenancy in a good set of chambers. I became conspicuously successful early on, and my practice and reputation grew quickly.

But success was underpinned by a working lifestyle that will be familiar to many, if not all. I was regularly working 60, 70 or more hours a week. I would pride myself on performing on just five or six hours sleep a night, regularly creeping into bed to delight in the pleasure of a long day's work well done. Social contacts and family life took second place. When I arrived home on a Friday evening, boxes of papers for the weekend were usually lined up either side of the doorway, heralding my arrival like an adoring crowd.

I became a distracted family man. Absent even when present, my mind was always working through the next case, my eye was always on the clock, jealously guarding my work time from the demands of intruding loved ones. My physical health started to suffer, with my weeks punctuated by regular back problems, frequent digestive issues, and when I was particularly tired, a twitching right eye. On the rare occasions of no weekend work, the time was spent recovering. Like a patient in the emergency room, I would escape from the trauma of the working week, emerging on Monday morning patched up for the days ahead.

Yes, I was conspicuously successful.

Eventually the inevitable happened – my mental and emotional wellbeing took a dive. I became desperately unhappy with the life I was leading. I had the earnings, the mansion house, the cars, the holidays, children in private schools, lavish parties with seemingly adoring friends, an enviable professional reputation – everything that many aspire to. But none of it was enough to compensate for the unending pressure and exhaustion of relentless work. I felt locked in. I tried to work out a different way of living with my wife of that time, but with hindsight I realize that we were both in patterns of behavior that at the time we were unable to change. In 2014, I became a QC, my marriage broke down, and by November I had left my beautiful home and broke up the family that I loved.

Throughout this period, to the best of my knowledge, my professional performance never faltered. My practice was booming. The accolades continued. And so in one sense everything was as it should be. But there was yet more to come. One evening in the following month, as I sat on a train out of London to travel to Newcastle for a week's work on a particularly challenging case, it happened. With no warning, I collapsed.

I remember it well from its aftermath. As I came around, three train stewardesses in their bright red uniforms had surrounded me, while a doctor who happened to be in the same carriage tightly squeezed my finger in a vain attempt to elicit some response. I lent them a confused gaze, then drifted back into unconsciousness once more, finally coming around a second time to an even larger crowd. Restored to an upright position, I remember looking across the table to my junior colleague who looked petrified – whether at my condition, or at the thought of having to handle the case on his own, I did not dare ask.

The doctor told me to get checked out in a hospital, but I was having none of that. After all, I had work to do. So I turned to my junior and asked what time we were due to start the following morning. "Nine o'clock," he stuttered. Without a second thought I replied, "Well, can you email the client and tell them we will start at ten instead, because I need to have a little rest". And then came a wonderful moment for which I am forever grateful. It was the moment when my junior – then newly qualified – gave me permission to be vulnerable, to be less than perfect. "What do you think you are doing?" he said. "You've just been told to go to hospital. You shouldn't be working at all." He showed me the leadership that I lacked at that time.

I returned to London the next day and went straight to bed. As I lay there, the familiar voices started their well-rehearsed dialogue: "It can't go on like this, things have to change, maybe you should quit, next time something serious could happen..." But this time I started to listen, not just because of the impact that work was having on me, but because it had now impacted on my ability to do my job. Whichever way I turned, I was in a bind. So I started to ask myself, "Why am I working like this?" and "How can I work differently?" A friend had been kind enough to give me the number of a systemic coach, which I had stored in my phone. I called it. I have never looked back.

The next half-decade was a relentless pursuit of answers to these questions, questions that I still keep in mind today. I undertook a great deal of personal inner work, identifying, acknowledging, understanding and resolving behavioral patterns from my past that were unsupportive in my present. I learnt to respect, value, and listen to my body, my feelings, and my intuition, just the same way as I had always respected, valued, and listened to my intellect. I trained and practiced in ways to integrate my whole self, including yoga, meditation, and phenomenology. And I started to look at my place through a systemic lens, so that I could better understand the various hidden forces and loyalties in play in my personal and professional realms.

As I started to draw up a new map to guide my life, I dared myself to question many of the rules, customs, and habits that govern legal practice, and the coded rules of the legal tribe that govern belonging and exclusion.[7] The hidden forces of belonging and exclusion are among the most powerful systemic forces in any human system. Depending on the context, they can be highly resourceful and supportive, or they can be debilitating and obstruct change. We see them in operation wherever people share a common purpose – among fraternity members, within sports teams, firms, families, professional associations, religions, war veterans and so on. The UK's struggle with Brexit is a modern example on an international scale. Because they are so well embedded, and often hidden in the subconscious, they create blind spots that can keep individuals and organizations stuck, without them realizing why. So coaching for change often involves revealing and attending to them in an appropriate, respectful way. These forces explain why many lawyers are reluctant to speak out about wellbeing or stress – to do so risks stigma and exclusion.

These are the rules that come with the hidden message, "This is what lawyers do, so if you want to be a real lawyer, this is what you must do too".

I was no longer interested in blindly following the customary wisdom that various hardships had to be endured as "life at the Bar". I was far more interested in finding ways of doing things that actually worked, and ultimately finding out how improving my wellbeing could enhance my professional practice.

This journey eventually brought me back to a joyful engagement with legal practice, and the process was so resourceful that I became committed to supporting others who were seeking change in their practices too. Fast forward to the present day, and I now divide my time between my legal practice and work as a systemic coach.

So, having got to this point, what was there to see?

Wellbeing and the upskilling of lawyers

What I saw then, and see more clearly now, is that wellbeing interventions – specifically, those interventions that are effective at increasing personal development and hence personal mastery – present a rich seam of opportunity for upskilling lawyers. The subject could fill a book in its own right. Out of necessity I have chosen three broad areas to illustrate the point.

Master yourself, master others

Self-awareness is not a trait commonly associated with the typical lawyer. There is a natural tendency to fool ourselves about our own professional proficiency – so-called "illusory superiority" – since it enhances our sense of self-worth.[8] For those lawyers that are serious about their wellbeing, they must move into a new territory. They have to point the finger inwards. They have to start with their own self.

Why? Because whatever wellbeing issues a person faces, they will be influenced, perhaps decisively, by their behavioral patterns. We see these patterns often when coaching. For example, a lawyer complains of over-work, yet feels unable to turn any new work away, despite being at breaking point. Intellectually gifted though they are, they are unable to break this cycle of paradoxical behavior. Often turning away work is associated with feelings of guilt or inadequacy, while taking on work is associated with feelings of competence and self-worth, particularly when clients express appreciation. The behavior continues, despite the long-term adverse effect on the lawyer's overall wellbeing.

Often changing these patterns of behavior is challenging because they are deeply embedded in relationship dynamics established in formative stages of life. In the example above, patterns of behavior like this might arise as a result a childhood lacking in expressions of love and support from a parent. Faced with an apparently cold, distant, or unhappy parent, the child sets about devising means of trying to get close to their parent, making them happy, and pleasing them in order to receive love, acknowledgment, and approval. This can lead to a pattern of behavior where the child sacrifices his or her own needs in order to try and please others. Personal boundaries become blurred. The reward of approval, if it ever comes, affirms that the pattern of behavior is worthwhile and leads to it being repeated. This cycle of behavior will only change once the individual has attended to their internal housekeeping and the influences of their family system that keep them stuck. The coaching journey of many lawyers and non-lawyers who present with issues such as stress, anxiety, over-work, fear of failure, perfectionism, insecurity, or low self-esteem or low self-esteem will often be more successful if the client is open to some consideration of their family dynamics. There are of course other helpful approaches - each person will have different needs, and it is always important to meet the client where they are in their own journey.[9]

So, how can addressing behavioral patterns upskill lawyers? There are three simple examples I would highlight.

First, since behavioral patterns are by their nature repetitive and somewhat automatic, addressing them frees up the lawyer to be more purposeful and conscious in their behavior. This is an important skill. An angry, aggressive person may well make a splendidly aggressive lawyer. But if the case does not call for aggression, what then? The ability to be purposeful in our approach to different clients, different witnesses, different judges and different opponents, to bring to the case the attitudes and behaviors that best meet the needs of the case and those of the client, is a valuable facet of successful lawyering. It is difficult to achieve while lawyers remain servient to unresolved personal issues that affect their working style.

Client relations are supported too. In the example of the over-worked lawyer given above, a successful coaching outcome would see the lawyer better able to delegate work to others without a sense of shame or inadequacy, and able to confidently discuss the client's needs with them openly and transparently, so that their work is undertaken by the lawyer or firm in a more effective way. Alternatively, the lawyer may simply say "no" to work because they are already at full stretch, and further work would prejudice the client's interests. Clients certainly value clear professional boundaries, transparent communication, and a genuine client-centered approach.

Secondly, once we have an awareness and understanding of our own patterns, we become far more adept at spotting and understanding other people's. This includes our opponents, the witness we have to cross-examine, or the difficult client that we have to contend with. When people are acting out patterns, their behavior becomes predictable – there is a kind of psychological "click-whirr".[10] In more extreme cases, such as when someone is triggered, they become completely unskilled.[11] This gives a profoundly effective weapon to the skilled lawyer who can recognize other people's triggers and knows how to pull them. Not only do they come to the fray well-armed, they have the capacity to disarm others.

Thirdly, addressing one's own patterns cultivates a mindset of self-inquiry and growth that is hugely resourceful during the course of one's professional life. Whereas a commonly observed professional path is from youthful vigor towards a steady, narrowing decline, a growth mindset means that we can remain agile practitioners for longer.[12]

Think systemically

One of my favorite stories to illustrate systemic thinking is a well-known one and goes something like this.[13] A woman is walking along a riverbank one day, and sees a baby floating by in the water. Quickly she rushes to the water's edge, leans across and saves the crying toddler from certain death. As she dries and comforts him, another baby bobs past, and so she calls to another passer-by who comes to the baby's aid and saves the second toddler from a similar fate. But no sooner is the second baby out of the water than a third appears, and so on, and before long the riverbank is filled with babies being tended by well-meaning passers-by. Some kind souls build a shelter, others buy food, and before long there stands an orphanage that is manned 24/7, fishing babies out of the water and caring for their wellbeing.

Then one day, a lady walks by, inspects the building, turns to the adults and says in a gentle but firm voice, "Isn't it about time you went upstream and found out who's throwing the babies in?"

I have already explained the importance of systemic thinking in resolving behavioral issues that can adversely impact lawyers. In what other ways does this type of thinking support wellbeing and professional performance? Here are three examples.[14]

First, systemic thinking supports the clear definition of roles within a team or organization. Roles are simply places within a relationship system. When a team of lawyers from different departments comes together to work on a transaction, or lawyers, witnesses, and support staff come together to litigate a trial, they form a relationship system. Well-defined roles give people a clear understanding of their responsibilities, their tasks, and their place within the team. By contrast, poorly defined roles lead to confusion over responsibilities, and can result in people unwittingly being drawn into inner or secret roles (such as a rescuer or carer), which can add to personal stress. For the same reasons, well-defined roles also support excellence in overall team performance.[15] Anyone who follows team sport will know that the well-functioning whole is greater than the sum of the parts.

Secondly, systemic thinking helps separate the individual from the role. Roles are not to be confused with the person who happens to be filling the role. This is important to wellbeing and professional performance because, when roles are personalized, the role holder and those around them tend to expect that everything required by that role will be performed by them and them alone. This can place huge and unrealistic burdens on the person concerned. By de-personalizing roles, lawyers and firms can more clearly understand the needs of the firm, the transaction or the litigation area, and what additional resources might be called upon to support those needs. De-personalization can also help lawyers separate their personal emotions from the task in hand, which in turn can soften the influence of unsupportive personal patterns of behavior.

Thirdly, systemic thinking can open up novel frontiers that can prove resourceful in legal practice. One example is the use of space. Spatial ordering is an important aspect of human systems. Lawyers are intuitively familiar with this – judges sit at the front of the court on a raised platform, parties sit lower and to the sides (claimants have their side and defendants have the other), while witnesses have a particular place to sit or stand when giving evidence. This spatial ordering supports the systemic orders within the courtroom. We intuitively sense its power and respond to it.

Space can be used in legal practice too. If as the lead lawyer in a team you sit at the head of the table when conducting a team conference, you will charge that space with authority. If, later in the meeting, you want to empower members of your team who are responsible for particular aspects of the case, try swapping places with them while they take the lead for that part of the meeting. The same can be done for conferences with teams of expert witnesses, where each expert can be asked to occupy the head of the table for their part of the meeting. Spatial mapping using systemic coaching tools can also be used to simplify complex problems and enhance case preparation and understanding.[16]

Employ the full self

Law schools and law training programs good at teaching law. They generally fail of skills needed to be an effective lawyer.[17] Law teaching and lawyer recruitment places huge emphasis on the value of logic, intellectual rigor, and verbal precision, much less on what is sensed, felt, or communicated by non-verbal means.

One of the benefits of enhancing wellbeing is the connection it gives you to your entire self, which in turn opens up a wider skillset to support some of the basic tasks involved in successful lawyering. Again, I give three examples.

First, improving wellbeing through adopting mindfulness-related practices can increase a lawyer's capacity to self-regulate, and hence stay well-resourced, present, and focused on the job.[18] Conscious breathing and breath control is well known to have this effect among those who practice it, and the science is now catching up with observed experience.[19] Yoga and meditation are simple means of cultivating this useful practice and increasing body awareness. The greater body awareness that these kinds of practices bring can also cultivate greater trust and accuracy in the body's capacity to inform.[20] Mindfulness can be challenging where personal issues remain unresolved, but it also provides a route to their resolution.[21]

Secondly, effective rapport building is a key step in communication and involves an awareness of how we bring our full selves into our communication. Rapport building involves not only the words we use to communicate, but the voice's pitch, tone, and pace; our body stance, use of signals and gesticulations, our capacity for subtle mirroring of others, and so on. Evidence suggests that communication styles can have a major influence on the likelihood of being the subject of a malpractice suit.[22] Greater body awareness increases our ability to understand how we are communicating and how we can enhance our communication skills.

Third, greater body self-awareness leads to greater awareness of others' non-verbal communication. Being receptive to non-verbal communication clues, and having some understanding of them, can be a valuable tool in lawyering because much non-verbal communication is subconscious. This means that it can give insights into attitudes and thought processes that the speaker may otherwise wish to hide, and otherwise hidden meanings may be revealed by identifying an incongruity between what is being said and the body language accompanying it.[23] To give a simple example, in one case I was involved in I was cross-examining an expert who was predicting the impacts of a proposed development on the local environment. When explaining the basis of his opinion he moved his hand to his chest. I cross-examined him on what that movement meant to him and why he had done it,[24] eventually getting the concession that his opinion was largely based on "a kind of heartfelt feeling," rather than objective evidence.

Conclusions

The legal profession faces the challenge of maintaining the wellbeing of its lawyers and ensuring that they remain competitive, capable, and service-orientated. These objectives should no longer be seen as pulling in opposite directions. There is now an opportunity for lawyers and law firms to draw new maps of what skillful and sustainable legal practice looks like in the 21st century. Wellbeing interventions that upskill lawyers can play a central role in supporting the profession and the clients that it serves. Excellence and wellbeing go hand in hand.

References

1. Member of the Middle Temple, Barrister-at-Law, Francis Taylor Building, Inner Temple, London; MA (Cambridge), LLM (London), FRSA, Visiting Professor of Law, King's College London; ORSC trained systemic coach, systemic constellations coach, NLP Master Practitioner, Member of the International Coaching Federation; co-founder (together with systemic coach Zita Tulyahikayo) of The Libra Partnership (www.thelibrapartnership.com), co-author, "Loving Legal Life" (on www.thelawyer.com).
2. A phrase coined by the Polish mathematician and philosopher, Alfred Korzybksi, whose work on general semantics have influenced language-based therapies and systemic thought: see Bandler and Grinder, *The Structure of Magic* (Science and Behavior Books Inc, 1975), chapter 1; Gregory Bateson, "Mind and Nature – A Necessary Unity" (Hampton Press, 2002), pp.27-28.
3. As Bateson, op. cit., says, "Korzybski's statement asserts that in all thought or perception or communication about perception, there is a transformation, a coding, between the report and the thing reported".

4. See J. Kim Wright, "Lawyers as Changemakers – the Global Integrative Law Movement" (American Bar Association, 2016).
5. In my first five years as Queen's Counsel I was nominated QC of the Year in my specialist area by the *Legal 500* directory three times, most recently for 2019. As a junior I was nominated four times for the prestigious Chambers and Partner's Junior Barrister of the Year award, and won it twice. I was ranked number one for several consecutive years in *Planning Magazine*'s annual review of the planning Bar. I add these biographical details to confront any conscious or subconscious bias that wellbeing is incompatible with professional excellence, and to dispel the more straightforward concern that I may not understand what professional excellence really involves. I believe I do understand it.
6. Systemic coaching looks through a systemic lens. This means that individual clients are coached within the context of their personal, family, cultural, and other systems that influence their loyalties, values, and behavior patterns; and teams and organizations are coached with the focus on their immediate and wider relationship system. In either case the work is underpinned by an understanding of the factors that influence how human systems naturally operate, including the instant relationship of the present moment with both past and future (ancient Greek **καιρός**, or kairos time).
7. For a description of some of these rules, see Pereira and Tulyahikayo, "Making the Change to Being Well" (*Counsel Magazine*, June 2018).
8. For an excellent account of psychological biases and other self-related impediments to a lawyer's development, see Randall Kiser's *Soft Skills for the Effective Lawyer* (CUP, 2017), chapter 3.
9. This is not a chapter on coaching, so I do not explain the details of coaching here. Skillful systemic coaching is holistic and solutions-focused, so it can deliver a speedy and lasting resolution to personal issues that impinge professional performance in a way that psychotherapy does not. Psychotherapy has an important role in cases of extreme trauma.
10. "Click-whirr" is the handy expression used by Cialdini to express the triggering of subconscious patterns of behavior in the context of the brain's susceptibility to influence; see Cialdini, Influence, *The Psychology of Persuasion* (Collins, 2007).
11. The triggered self is associated with the adult becoming hijacked by dysfunctional childhood behavioral patterns. As Anais Nin has written, "We do not grow absolutely, chronologically. We grow sometimes in one dimension, and not in another; unevenly. We grow partially. We are relative. We are mature in one realm, childish in another. The past, present, and future mingle and pull us backward, forward, or fix us in the present."
12. The discovery of the neuro-plasticity of the brain has confirmed that even old dogs can learn new tricks.
13. Abridged from J. Kim Wright, op. cit., p.87, which attributes it to David Lamotte, *World Changing 101: Challenging the Myth of Powerlessness* (Motreat, NC: Dryad Publishing, 2014).

14. There are many layers and aspects to systems thinking and it permeates a huge variety of subject areas. The three simple examples given here are three of a vast number that could have been given.
15. For more detail, see Pereira and Tulyahikayo, "Do you know your role?" *The Lawyer*, 7 June 2019.
16. The use of paper constellations from systemic coaching can be used can be used to map out case dynamics and understand how changes to those dynamics will impact on the problem at hand.
17. Kiser, op. cit. at p.24, "Very little information about the skills required to excel in law practice has been obtained, and to the extent information has been compiled, it has little effect on law school curricula and continuing education programmes".
18. "Proper breathing brings better health," *Scientific American*, January 2019.
19. A good starting point for resources and learning is the Mindfulness in Law Society (MILS) of the United States: www.mindfulnessinlawsociety.com.
20. Greater discussion of this topic is beyond the scope of this chapter, but everyone is familiar with the idea of "feeling" that something is wrong or right, particularly in the gut. Indeed, many clients ask lawyers for their "gut feel" to particularly complicated problems.
21. Research suggests that malpractice suits are far less likely against negligent medical practitioners who are good communicators compared to those who are not: Malcolm Gladwell, *Blink* (Penguin, 2006), pp.40-43. The importance of lawyer wellbeing is now a focus of the legal insurance industry: see, *Why the Legal Sector Must Tackle Mental Health*, Adam Riley, Director, Head, Legal Sector Practice Employee Benefits and Wellbeing, Howden Group (published on LinkedIn, 18 June 2019).
22. See Bessel Van Der Kolk, The Body Keeps the Score (Penguin, 2014), pp208-210.
23. For a general exposition of how word choice and non-verbal cues can reveal the mental representational system of the speaker, see Bandler and Grinder, *The Structure of Magic II* (Science and Behavior Books, 1976).
24. Coaching frequently explores inner feelings and thoughts by "unfolding" physical channels of communication in collaboration with the client. Because the physical movement is a fact that has happened, it cannot be disputed, and because it has happened subconsciously, it tends to connect to an inner truth that is difficult for the person concerned to deny.

Chapter 12: When altruism is not enough – the economics of wellbeing in the legal profession

By Renee Branson, founder, RB Consulting

Lawyers in the UK, Australia, Europe, and the United States have something in common – rates of depression, anxiety, substance abuse, and suicide are higher in the legal than most other professions. Globally, over recent years, the legal industry has taken notice of its rising mental health crisis. Awareness campaigns and initiatives have been launched with efforts to decrease the stigma associated with seeking mental health care. Mindfulness and meditation are being lauded as ways to mitigate the stress of the job and some law firms even offer benefits such as on-site counseling for those in crisis. In the UK, LawCare, a charity organization providing mental health and wellbeing information and resources to the legal profession, has seen a steady increase in its crisis helpline calls. Citing the pressures of the billable hour, long hours that impact sleep and health, and an adversarial environment, the charity does not envision those calls slowing down. That's why other organizations like the American Bar Association in the US and the MindsCount Foundation in Australia have begun to build frameworks for improved wellbeing and resilience within firms. Joseph Fournier, president of the talent advisory and executive search firm InveniasPartners, notes that other industries have embraced wellbeing as worthy of investment. He cites Deloitte and JPMorgan as companies that invest in wellbeing. Even the World Economic Forum in Davos, Switzerland, recognizes "integrated wellbeing" (physical, emotional, social, and financial) as an economic driver. These are critical strides toward improved mental health within the industry. Why, then, is measurable cultural change still lagging?

Awareness campaigns require a lower level of buy-in than does a commitment to systemic change. Elizabeth Rimmer, chief executive of LawCare, is encouraged by the dramatic increase in requests they receive from law firms seeking training. However, she continues on to say that when it comes to law firms operationalizing wellbeing within the firm, a "gap exists between awareness and strategy". Awareness occurs at the contemplation and determination stages of change, before action actually takes place. "We are in the pioneering stage of this movement," she explains. The ABA's *Pathway to Lawyer Wellbeing* articulates the reality that systemic change can only occur when there is "broad scale buy-in" for action from top leadership in law firms, law schools, and bar associations. How can the legal profession be motivated to challenge long-standing norms in order to prioritize mental wellbeing? The most common appeal, one of altruism and morality – that it is simply the right thing to do – is not enough on its own to create the necessary sea change.

A continuous process

In 2016, the American Bar Association formed the Wellbeing Task Force, which issued a report on lawyer wellbeing in 2018. The taskforce defined lawyer wellbeing as a continuous process in which lawyers strive for thriving in each of the six dimensions of their lives – emotional, occupational, social, intellectual, spiritual, and physical. The ABA also created the Wellbeing Pledge, calling on legal employers to recognize that substance abuse and mental health problems constitute a significant challenge in the legal profession. Signatories are encouraged to pledge their support to improve mental wellbeing in their workplaces. To help accomplish this, the ABA provided actionable steps to cultivate the mental wellbeing of legal professionals that correlate to the seven-point framework. The ABA taskforce's goal was to have all legal employers sign onto the pledge by 1 January 2019. However, there have been just 164 legal employers (firms, legal departments, and law schools) who have signed as of January 2020, a full year beyond the original goal. These strides are to be lauded, and yet it is becoming increasingly clear that there needs to be a business case made for wellbeing and not simply an altruistic one. Fortunately, it is not a difficult case to make.

According to the World Health Organization (WHO), depression, anxiety, and substance abuse is said to cost the global economy $1 trillion annually in lost productivity. Within the legal industry, rates of depression, anxiety, and substance abuse are close to four times the rate than in other professions, making the lion's share of the $1 trillion loss likely to fall within the legal domain. Absenteeism and "presenteeism" (employees who are physically at work, but are unable to fully function) create economic strain on otherwise successful enterprises. The cost goes beyond lost productivity, however. Untreated mental illness and substance dependence are associated with higher rates of heart disease, diabetes, chronic pain, and other costly medical conditions. Investing in wellbeing through initiatives, programming, and benefits is shown to yield a large return. The WHO shows that for every $1 invested in the treatment of common mental health disorders, there is a $4 return on investment in improved health and productivity.

The cost of attrition

Beyond absenteeism and presenteeism are the high rates of attrition in the legal profession, particularly of associates. The costs incurred from lawyers who leave their jobs (or the profession altogether) can significantly cut into a law firm's profit margin. According to the National Association of Legal Placement (NALP), 44 percent of all associates in the US, both entry-level and lateral hires, leave their firms within three years. Attrition rates are as high as 81 percent in the first five years for entry-level associates, according to JD Match and Right Profile. Reasons cited for departure include intense time demands, toxic work culture (including bullying and harassment), and lack of professional–personal life balance. How does this translate to cost? By JD Match and Right Profile estimates, replacement costs are one-and-a-half to two times the departing lawyer's compensation. This can quickly cost a firm USD400,000 (£0.31m/ 0.36m) or more for each associate who leaves. Considering current attrition rates, the annual cost of this loss in a 500-lawyer firm could reach USD34 million. Pulling the lens back further, USD9.1 billion is lost annually to attrition in the top 400 firms in the United States alone.

Then there are the harder-to-quantify contributors to profitability loss. In a joint study by the ABA Commission on Lawyer Assistance Programs and the Hazelden Betty Ford Foundation, 40 to 70 percent of all disciplinary and malpractice hearings involved lawyer depression, anxiety, substance abuse, or a combination of these factors. This translates to monetary loss directly related to the malpractice; firms also sustain damage to morale, productivity, and reputation that indirectly impacts profit. Even without lawyer behaviors slipping into the realm of malpractice, clients are becoming more attuned to the quality of work (or lack thereof) by frayed-nerved, sleep-deprived attorneys. Recently, a partner of an Atlanta law firm shared that he received a phone call from a client one morning. The client reported getting an email from an associate time-stamped 2:35 am. "*You might think that the time of the email impressed me or showed me the associate's dedication,*" said the client, "*but it didn't. It worried me. No one is any good at 2:35 am.*" The client cares little that the associate was trying to meet a 2,000 billable hour target for the year. The client cares about having a lawyer they can trust to protect their interests through the quality of their work.

The billable hour helps to perpetuate a system that discourages efficiency and encourages the churn and burn that results in middle-of-the-night emails. A cynical view of lawyer attrition rates is that it is simply the collateral damage to an otherwise profitable model. And while the billable hour is still king, more clients are seeking alternative fee arrangements that promote efficiency and productivity. Long hours, which are the norm with the billable hour, do not equal productivity; indeed, quite the opposite. A study published in the *American Journal of Epidemiology* showed that those who worked just 15 hours more than the traditional 40-hour work week scored lower on cognitive tests measuring short-term memory and fluid intelligence, such as problem solving and abstract thinking. It goes without saying, these cognitive functions are critical to lawyers' abilities to practice their craft. Management consultant Tim Corcoran reports that:

> *"While private practice lawyers tend to recognize how unhappy the billable hour model makes their clients, it persists because the lawyers think it's good for them. It's not and never has been. While other businesspeople rely on their expertise to generate profits while they sleep, lawyers seek profits from working ever-longer hours, which is the exact opposite of profiting from experience. This is why the legal market is ripe for competitive disruption."*

If we can take away the incentive to bill ten hours for a job that could be done in six, we will have more lawyers at their functional best – physically, mentally, and emotionally.

Investing in wellbeing

Once the decision is made to invest in wellbeing initiatives, how do law firms ensure that they have a professional who is able to produce outcomes and returns on that investment? With few road maps or even a clear definition of what a "wellbeing professional" is, it can be difficult to determine the right fit for a particular firm's needs. These professionals come from a variety of backgrounds, can be credentialed in vastly different things, and have a wide breadth of knowledge and experience. They are licensed therapists, social workers, personal coaches, nurses, mindfulness experts, and even personal fitness trainers. Each bring their own unique talents to the table. While there is a place for all of these talents within the larger framework of wellbeing, there are four key elements that an organization should look for when bringing in a professional to design and head a wellbeing program.

- **Systemic understanding.** A wellbeing professional who works within any organization is working within a system. That system creates the culture, structure, hierarchy, and institutional history. Those elements, in turn, have significant impact on the lived experience of those who work there. This is particularly true in law firms that have markedly different structures and cultures from other professions. A professional's ability to identify and properly assess how the larger system bolsters or inhibits individual wellbeing increases their ability to create programming that improves not only the wellness of individual attorneys, but productivity, achievement, and wellbeing of the firm as a whole. To make a medical parallel, a doctor can treat the symptoms of a child's asthma attack and the child has momentary relief. When she also enquires about the child's environment, such as exposure to second-hand smoke, the doctor can assist in providing resources such as smoking cessation programs that positively impact the child's long-term as well as the health of the entire family system.
- **Continuum of care.** In chapter 11, James Pereira relates the parable about people standing beside a riverbank when they notice a baby drowning in the rushing current. Eventually, one rescuer realizes that they can't keep pulling drowning babies out of the water, and the real solution is to go upstream and find out who is throwing the babies in. Understanding continuum of care means being able to provide or refer to programming and services that range from proactive and preventative (stopping whoever is throwing babies in the river), to restorative treatment and care (pulling them out when they go in). A professional skilled in addiction recovery or physical fitness plays a vital (and even life-saving) role within a wellbeing framework. Such a targeted area of expertise, however, might not best serve a director's role that requires wholistic programming along the continuum of care.
- **Knowledge of industry standards**. More and more industry associations are creating standards of wellbeing as a guide to their member organizations. The American Bar Association's Wellbeing Pledge and Toolkit was born out of the 2017 ABA National Task Force on Lawyer Wellbeing. Some of these guidelines are just that – suggested guidelines. Others, like the ABA Pledge and Toolkit

encourage law firms to become signatories to the pledge and commit to specific standards. A wellbeing professional within the legal industry should have a deep understanding of the seven pillars of the ABA Wellbeing Pledge, best practices for attorneys and legal professionals, and strategies for not only meeting, but exceeding, those standards.

- **Use of assessment and evaluation.** You can't repair what you don't know is broken. Many times we know *something* is wrong, but the exact "what" can be harder to determine. When the water starts dripping from the kitchen ceiling, we know we have a problem. What precisely is causing that leak and getting it fixed requires a call to the plumber. A wellbeing professional should have the ability to evaluate an organization's challenges *and* strengths through skilled observation, interviewing, and formal diagnostic assessment. Furthermore, they should have the ability to set targeted outcomes and collect data on those outcomes for evaluation.

As with any professional position within a law firm, there is no one-size-fits-all. Having a strong foundation in the four key areas above ensures that the professional you hire or train to lead a wellbeing initiative has solid footing to meet your law firm's unique needs.

There must be a continued appeal to the moral and ethical case for improving the wellbeing of lawyers and other professionals who are negatively impacted by an often-punishing career. It truly is the right thing to do. But we must also couple that altruistic appeal with a solid business case and vetted leadership that provides justification for long-term financial and structural investments in wellbeing.